from BROKE *to* BREAD WINNER

Advance Praise

Chakravarthy's story is compelling and powerful. Through her personal and professional experience, she is uniquely equipped to help and advise Indian women facing divorce and a future as a single mom. However, her ingredients to live by apply to single moms the world over, regardless of country or culture. Her strength and practical wisdom shine through in this book. With a forward-looking focus, Chakravarthy shows the reader how to move on with her life while making it fulfilling for herself and her children. I also love her "Guardian-Mom Philosophy" (i.e., moving from a feeling of ownership towards her children to becoming a guardian-mom where she instead had a responsibility to nourish and cherish them as a delegate for God/the Universe). A must-read for single moms everywhere, *From Broke to Breadwinner* will give you the courage, conviction, and confidence to believe in yourself—if Chakravarthy could do it, so can you!

—**Sunny Joy McMillan**, author of
Unhitched: Unstick Your Bad Marriage

I could relate completely with Janaki's story, so much so that I cried while reading many of the chapters. Her book *From Broke to Breadwinner* speaks from the heart right from the beginning. It is a remarkably well written and helpful book, with advice that comes from living through the experience of divorcing, trying to find her new way in the world, becoming the best mom she can be, and providing for her family. Those who are going through the experience will find many helpful pearls of wisdom.

—**Katie Coates**, author of *Yes Vote:*
The Public Hearing Plan for Developers

Spot on, personal, insightful. I wish I had this book 20 years ago to guide me in my single parent journey. I especially appreciate the five principle of being a guardian mother- redefining what traditional roles and loving your children look like. Great Book!

—**Dr. Kate Dow**, Anxiety Coach and author of
Fear-Less: The Art of Using Anxiety to Your Advantage

The Single Mom's Guide to Financial Independence and More

Janaki Chakravarthy

NEW YORK
LONDON • NASHVILLE • MELBOURNE • VANCOUVER

from **BROKE** *to* **BREADWINNER**
The Single Mom's Guide to Financial Independence and More

Published in New York, New York, by Morgan James Publishing in partnership with Difference Press. Morgan James is a trademark of Morgan James, LLC.
www.MorganJamesPublishing.com

The Morgan James Speakers Group can bring authors to your live event. For more information or to book an event visit The Morgan James Speakers Group at www.TheMorganJamesSpeakersGroup.com.

ISBN 978-1-64279-022-1 paperback
ISBN 978-1-64279-023-8 eBook
Library of Congress Control Number: 2018937005

Cover Design by:
Rachel Lopez
www.r2cdesign.com

Interior Design by:
Bonnie Bushman
The Whole Caboodle Graphic Design

This book is dedicated to its heroes:
single moms the world over.

TABLE OF CONTENTS

INTRODUCTION

"I wanted books to change me, and I wanted to write books that would change others."

—**Jack Gantos**, Hole in My Life

Books have always been my source of inspiration. I am an introvert and books have been my best friends in good and bad times. They have provided me wisdom, and answers to abstract questions. They have consoled and inspired me and given me valuable tools to improve myself and live a better life. My wish for you, my reader, is that this book does the same for you.

I took on the role of a single mom when I was in my early thirties. It was the early 1990s and I lived in Bangalore in South India. I had two daughters who were 12 and 10 years old then. Becoming a single mom in my day and age came with a lot of social stigma and quite a bit of unchartered territory to navigate for me—professionally on a job and career front, and personally on the home management and emotional front of being a single parent. It took many hard knocks, growing pains, significant emotional and psychological fortification and reorientation, and, finally, a really thick skin to get through those initial years of being a single mom. I had to change and recalibrate my own expectations for my daughters and myself and what I expected from others and the world around me to get through those years. From a hardworking but broke homemaker, I had to become a tough career-seeking breadwinner for my family while also retaining the space to be the *mom* my girls needed me to be. I had to help my daughters adjust and accept the single parent/mom household they were now in.

This book is about the perspectives, knowledge, and wisdom I gained. I'd like to share these with you so that your journey as a single mom can be a tad smoother, your load a wee bit lighter, and your heart and spirit more uplifted and free to fly higher.

SINGLE MOM–I KNOW YOU

"She has to have four arms, four legs, four eyes, two hearts, and double the love. There is nothing single about a single mom."
—Mandy Hale

Vidya's Story

My client Vidya lived in Mysore, India. She was 28, a happy and enterprising homemaker, with a five-year-old son Adi and her newborn daughter Aishu, when her husband Vinay announced to her that he was done with their marriage. Vinay had been traveling for work when the baby was born. He had visited her in the hospital and Vidya hadn't a clue about his intentions. But a fortnight later, he returned home from his next trip and made his declaration. There was no specific reason, though Vidya suspected that he had found somebody else. He did not even want their children. He left home and there was no other word from him. He had stopped her access to their joint bank account.

Vidya was devastated. She thought it was just a bad dream and things would be fine when she awoke. She could not believe that her marriage was over and kept reaching out to her husband and his family with the hope of reconciliation. She searched over and over in her mind for the possible reasons for the break-up and what she could have done or not done for her husband not to love her anymore and for him wanting to just leave her, the marriage, and the children.

After a few months of hoping and wishing, when there was still no sign of her husband, Vidya was forced to accept that she was now solely in charge of her children and that she had to start earning soon to be able to feed them. She had never worked in a professional space in her life before and had enjoyed being a homemaker. She was in a state of panic. Who would give her a job? She had a general Bachelor of Arts degree with no real specialization, but was that enough to find a job? Adi would soon go to school (in India, child education is not free for all) and Aishu needed baby things, so would she be able to earn enough for all this? Though her parents offered her their place, they were retired and lived on their modest retirement income, so where would she go if she did not want to be a burden on them? Her son was asking about his father and what would she tell him? How could she bring up a boy without a father? The neighbors were pointing fingers at her and either cluck-clucking or gossiping about how she could not hold on to her husband and she felt ashamed to walk by them.

Vidya felt totally demoralized and bereft. She was angry with her husband, God, everyone and everything. It was at this point of time that a mutual friend referred her to me.

Jaya's Journey

My client Jaya's story was different, yet similar. Jaya lived in Dallas with her husband Ramesh and two daughters, Vinu and Anu, aged 6 and

3. Her husband was in a good position in an Information Technology company and she held a part-time job as a pharmacist. Her salary went mostly to day-care for her children. The marriage was fraying at the edges because Ramesh thought that Jaya should stop working for the paltry salary, just stay put at home, and be a homemaker and mom. But Jaya enjoyed her career; it gave her independence and an identity outside of the home. And wasn't she also making use of her education and qualifications?

The marriage kept going downhill and there were violent arguments at home. The couple's quarrels were upsetting the children. Finally, Ramesh wanted to end the marriage. Jaya now faced the situation of having to pay for the divorce attorney and finding a job that would support her and her share of the children's care. What had been almost a hobby now had to be her livelihood. She had to find a new place to live with her daughters. She had lost most of her friends—who were divided in their loyalties between her and Ramesh—and had chosen him over her. Jaya reached out to me at this stage in her life wondering how she was going to move forward and survive.

Lata's Tale

Another client of mine, Lata, lived in Mumbai, India. Lata and her husband Trilok had a five-year-old son, Kumar. Lata had a General Arts degree and had done a beautician's course before getting married, but Trilok had insisted that she did not need to work outside of the home. Trilok liked parties where he drank a lot. His alcohol addiction soon progressed to drinking at home too. He was abusive to Lata when he was drunk. Lata's in-laws entreated her not to leave Trilok. After trying hard but unsuccessfully to cure Trilok of his addiction, and worried about their son's welfare, Lata sought legal recourse to end their marriage. She had physical and mental scars from her marriage: in trying to deal with Trilok's outbursts, in facing the shame of being verbally abused in front of her neighbors, in trying to cope with her in-laws' emotional pleas. She was also daunted at the prospect of stepping out as an earner. She was unsure her beautician qualification would earn her enough to pay for the household and her child's expenses. At this crossroads in her life, Lata got in touch with me and sought my advice and guidance to see her through.

Stories of Reality

Do you see yourself in the stories of these women? Unfortunately, they are typical of what an Indian woman has to go through when her breadwinning husband abandons or divorces her. Alternatively, if you courageously decide to get out of an unhappy marriage and seek a separation and/or divorce (as I did), you still have a long road ahead of you. The idea of a separation can be so overwhelming and paralyzing for so many reasons that you may go to great lengths or put up with almost anything rather than end the marriage.

So there is no sugar-coating it. Getting out of a marriage is rife with struggles and challenges. While the stories I have shared above are examples of situations and people from an Indian background, you as a single mom may face similar or different kinds of challenges, whatever part of the world you live in.

The Super Single Mom

When you are a single mom, you are like the Greek God Atlas, carrying the weight of the whole world on your shoulders. The analogy may be even more apt because your children are your world, and you are carrying the responsibility of their lives in your hands. So you are special, for the simple reason that while there were two people who participated in the creation of your children, there is now primarily only you to provide for, raise, and care for them.

It is especially hard if you, like me, have to change yourself from the role of homemaker to that of a home manager + breadwinner + societal warrior + child protector + single parent. Add to that, if you are starting late as an earner, you don't even know *where* you are going to *look*, let alone *find* a job, and *when* you are going to be earning enough to meet all your needs. You feel insecure about everything. You also carry emotional scars from the battles of the divorce and all that takes time to heal. It is a huge load for one human being to carry. It is like having to scale Mt. Everest when you have not yet hiked up the local butte.

So if you are new to this role as a single mom, who also has to be the breadwinner, please know that you are a Superwoman. You already are, before reading this book, before you understand what my messages are, before you adopt them. Just by virtue of the fact that you have taken on the primary responsibility of raising your children yourself, you deserve the pedestal of a superlative person.

However, it is often very hard for single moms to believe this. It is difficult to think of yourself as a hero while you are dealing with the multifarious responsibilities of your life and juggling your time every day between earning and caring for your children. You often think you are doing a poor job of everything. Sometimes you think you are doing an okay job. And rarely/almost never do you think you are doing a great job. This is because, as a mother, you want to be the best that you can be. You second-guess yourself, your thoughts, emotions, decisions, and actions in trying to see and do what is right for your family and your children. You often put yourself and your needs last. And it is this intrinsic approach to life and motherhood that takes a heavy toll when you become a *single* mother because now you are at it alone with no validation—and a lot of opposition—in every aspect of your life.

A Single Mom's Journey Anywhere

The Challenges

When you emerge from your divorce, you wonder why this ever happened to you and what really went wrong. You feel anger or you feel guilt—anger for the injustice of it all, guilt for your perceived inadequacies that made the marriage end. While you are going through the motions of your new life, a part of you is still living in the past, among recriminations, blame, regrets, and so on. You often hang on to lost hopes and dreams, struggling to let them go and build new ones for yourself.

Society adores happy marriages so much that it is hard to just deal with your new single status. Do I tell people that I am divorced/separated or not? Will they see me differently? How will it affect my life? How will my children get treated? How do I answer the question, "So what does your husband do?" Why can't what I do be enough for a conversation? While struggling with these basic, day-to-day human interactions and societal fitting-in issues, you have the larger, higher-stakes issues of earning money and raising children.

As a single mom, you have to be both mom and dad to your children in your home, even if the dad has shared responsibilities. You have to make sure they are safe while you work. You have to send them to school, make their meals, and care for them when they are sick. As a late-starting breadwinner, you might also not be able to afford all the nice things their dad could provide for them, so you feel insecure about your children's love. You have to re-baseline the hopes and dreams for them that you had as part of a married couple and live instead in survival mode. Your children will want both parents together and sometimes long for their dad. You have to answer their questions and explain why their parents are not together. Your children often don't understand you or why you do what you do—so at times it feels like you are fighting them. You have to be emotionally strong for yourself and your children.

The future at this point looks bleak. You are starting late in being employed or starting to earn. Where will you even find a job—and with possibly outdated or irrelevant qualifications, where will you start? Who can help you find a job? When will you earn enough to make all ends meet? How do you balance the necessity of working hard with the time and attention the children need? How do you improve your earning power among all these constraints? Monetary worries could plague you all night.

From a time management perspective, once you do come across that lucky break of being employed, you have to get used to a new routine, one that begins at home early in the day and ends late at night. This is a routine that makes you focus on working outside of the home for most of the day and then continue working at home with all the home chores. You need an abundance of energy. So where will you derive your strength? How do you recharge and sustain your physical and mental energy and effort?

Life at home and work forces you to learn new skills. Your job might require you to study and gain new knowledge when the children are in bed. You have to learn about numerous things on the job front to be or become competitive on the job market. This may require formal classes and certifications. You have to learn about retirement savings, baseline and variable pays, benefits, bonuses, advancement opportunities, and perks. You have to learn about the work culture even as you have to learn to advocate for yourself within it.

On the home front, you have to take over all the responsibilities and the work within and outside the house that your husband may have handled in the past. Attending to broken home appliances and dealing with the handyman may not have been chores that you would have had to do earlier, but now you have nobody but yourself to take care of such things. You constantly have an eye out for new ways to save money. You have to become street-smart so that you are not being conned by anyone and are able to adopt the cheapest, most durable, and most efficient and effective solution for any problem you face. You thought you were done with learning and exams and now all this?

Do you even have time to think about yourself? How do you find the time to just put your head down and rest? Even the small luxuries can seem unaffordable and you keep putting off indulging in any form of relaxation and recreation. How do you take care of your health? While you can't afford any form of downtime, you also think you can and have to somehow manage to keep your aching body up and about all the time. On the emotional front, who will support you, lift you up when needed, and cheer you on as you find the courage to live by your convictions? Who will console you when you feel guilty about something you were unable to do or when you are worried about so many things? Unfortunately, you are on your own, tackling and facing life with its unending demands and requirements.

You are tired. Hurt. Angry. Scared. And defensive. You often feel—and are—alone, as there isn't another adult in the house to discuss your thoughts and feelings with, bounce off your ideas, or share your joys, sorrow, or load with. How do you reorient yourself to this new chapter in your life? How can you deal with so much change in such a short period of life when everything looks stacked against you? How do you muster the energy and confidence required to move forward? And in all these struggles what do you hope for?

The Dreams

As a single mom, you wish the best for your children, everything their father would be able to give them. You want your child or children to be as secure as they would be with two parents. You want them not to miss their father. You desire what your two-parent friends' and neighbors' kids have. You want your kids to be safe and happy while you are earning for them. You want to be there for their big and little moments.

You want a job that pays well, that helps you provide for your children comfortably. You wish that your work would also give you time with your children. You desire a career that would make you feel confident and comfortable. You want to catch up on earning, on the lost years when you were a homemaker. You dream that you are successful and get a raise in your job. You want to advance in your career in the shortest possible time.

You wish for abundant mental and physical energy. You don't want to feel low and down. You want somebody to take away all the weight on your shoulders. You want miracles to happen and your life to look up. You want to throw away the despondence that envelops you day and night.

You wish that a genie would take care of all the things that you have to do in a day. You long for a mani-pedi and a relaxed day with your friends. You hope that some day you can afford to have a holiday.

In short, my dear reader, you want magic to be there in the world to take your troubles and worries away and center you with light, joy, and hopefulness. But most importantly, you dream that your children are proud of you and think you are the best mom they could ever have. You really want to be a Super Single Mom.

My Aspiration for You

My life as a single mom was like running an unending marathon for the dozen or so years till my daughters became independent adults. The days were full, the chores relentless, and my emotions always running on roller coaster rides, but there was a clear purpose in life: that of earning, caring, and enabling my children to be well-equipped adults in every way. I learned and grew myself as a parent, as an earner, and as a human being. I would not have traded my life as a single mom for anything else.

When I embarked on my single-mom life, I learned a few life lessons. Consciously or unconsciously, I adopted certain ingredients/principles to live by so that I could survive. These ingredients guided and energized my single-mom journey. They kept me on course, gave me strength when I was tired, and made me a better parent. They helped me recreate myself from a married, homemaker mom to a single, breadwinner mom who tried to be the best role model for her daughters. They have made up my recipe for success as a single mom.

This book is about those nuggets of wisdom that I gained. I have shared them with many clients as they made similar journeys and they have told me that these nuggets helped them greatly as they made their transitions into single-mom hood. I know times have changed and we see educated and employed Indian women in all walks of life, traveling all over the world, and transplanting themselves outside of India. But if you are divorced, separated, or considering separation by choice or force, and struggling to start your life as an earner, worrying about how you can be both a good parent and provider, then my heart goes out to you. I have written this book for you, to help you reinvent yourself into the breadwinner single mom.

My focus is not how or why your marriage ended, or is ending, but on how you should move forward with your life and make it wholesome and fulfilling for yourself and your children. My book is about healing from within and developing certain perspectives, habits, and attitudes to life as a single mom that will help you feel stronger and surer in your role and decision-making.

So, my dear reader, my wish for you is this: I hope my book gives you the courage, conviction, and confidence to believe in yourself—to truly find peace and feel strong and certain in the core of your being, to trust yourself and find the strength to achieve the great mission you have undertaken, and to successfully navigate this difficult journey. I hope the stories, learning, and the recipe I share with you offer you renewed purpose, energy, and tools to make the right decisions for you and your little ones. I hope it offers you the validation you need that you are doing the right things for your family as a single mom. And so I share my recipe with you in this book, hoping it helps you as it did my clients and me.

SUPER SINGLE MOM, I *AM* YOU

"Becoming a mother cannot help but change things."
—Sarah Zettel

The Life of an Indian Woman of My Generation

I was born in South India into a Hindu, middle class, Brahmin family. To describe the milieu of my generation of middle class women, we got educated and were also taught some form of fine arts—dance, classical music. The expectation was that we get married between your late teens and the early twenties. If you were still unmarried by the time you reached your mid-twenties, you were looked upon as a burden on your parents, and society wondered what was wrong with you that you couldn't land a man. This is true in many cultures even today where we expect women to be whole only if they have partnered up. In India, at that time, arranged marriages were the norm, and you would be lucky if you got to speak a few words with your fiancé before the wedding.

Joint families, where you lived with your husband along with your parents-in-law and brothers and sisters-in-law and their families, were very common, and in fact were the norm. The system worked because everybody had a designated role in the home, a pooling of resources, and inter-dependency among the different members of the household. As a result, it was important and expected that families from similar religious, social, and economical strata would come together to form an alliance for their children. The assumption was that this would make for a happier, conflict-free, smooth, more harmonious union and marriage. There would be no conflict in the values that one wanted to teach and raise the children with. Overall, the relationship was expected to be healthier, and, with the families' blessings and interventions as needed, the marriage would last.

As women and wives we were taught to be obedient, respectful of our husbands and the in-laws, to put up with troublesome situations, and be good homemakers. If women worked outside of the home, it was more a hobby than out of a need. Women's skills had to shine only at home. A good singer could provide the pleasure of her music only to her family and pass it on to her daughter. A smart, well-educated woman could be a part-time or full-time teacher and use her knowledge to teach her children. While the family she married into might be proud of her accomplishments, her light shone within the boundaries of her immediate family. Men were the designated providers. Fathers and husbands ruled the roost. It was a patriarchal system in a patriarchal society and women conformed—happily and sometimes unhappily. The ideal daughter-in-law and wife adjusted. She would be the pillar holding the whole family together. This was the picture painted and the position she was assigned to that many women like me tried to live up to.

Women in my time (and even today) lived through good and bad marriages. They had to put up with the husband's follies and foibles and find excuses to stay in the marriage. If your husband was a drunk, at least he didn't hit you. If your husband hit you, at least he didn't hurt the children. Women were not expected to even acknowledge any differences in needs or habits between them and their husbands such as lifestyle, relationship expectations and communication, personal values to raise children with, and worldviews to share with each other. They had to just follow the rules of the married household. Tolerance for the sake of society and for the sake of children was the virtue promoted and advocated to women.

Needless to say, divorces were almost unheard of. Divorced women and widows were second or third class citizens and divorced women were "bad." They were not invited to social occasions. They were gossip topics for other women. They were pointed at and whispered about. They were "forward" and hence looked upon as easy game for men. Other married women perceived them to be a threat to themselves. The parents of such women were pitied and blamed. The siblings of these women would find it hard to get married because one woman in the family did not have a successful marriage. There was a great deal of shame and struggle in being a divorcée.

So it was not easy to break out of the mold and make the decision of ending a marriage. What was more arduous was to take on the role of the breadwinner after being a homemaker; to enter yet another traditionally patriarchal setting and start earning; to progress to earning enough to be self-sufficient (as those traditional hobbies or avocations usually did not pay enough to support the life and family of a single mom); to do all of this while also dealing with family pressures and societal censure and, most importantly, while striving to be a good single parent. Life as a single mom required loads of motivation and strength.

My Story

I was the younger of two children, and my brother is two years older than me. My parents had intended that I should be educated, happily married, and have kids. In conformance to those standards, I obtained a Masters Degree in home science that would help me be a good homemaker. I wanted to pursue science like my older brother and had aspirations of earning and being employed, but those aspirations died a natural death as I grew to understand societal and parental expectations of me.

But when it came to marriage, I chose to rebel. I met my husband-to-be during the final year of my post-graduation and we decided to get married after a few months of courtship. He belonged to a different religion and community but we thought that those differences did not matter. Of course, this kind of love marriage was not very common in those days. My parents objected violently initially but since I was firm in my resolve to get married to him, they gave in and performed my wedding, as was the Indian custom. We got married right after my graduation. In India—and in most places in the world—parents participate in some form of ceremonial tradition where they give away their daughter to the groom, and, in the case of the India of those times, also to his family. As expected, my husband and I lived in a joint family with his parents and siblings. We had two daughters in the first four years of marriage. My daughters were named Nina and Divya.

In the first few years of marriage, I tried to fit in with my husband's family. I tried to do the usual things any new bride in an Indian joint family would do. I took lessons to learn my husband's family language, as it was different from mine. He and I communicated with each other in English. I put my home science degree to good use. I learned to cook the dishes that my married family was used to, to conform to their traditions. I tried to be a good wife, daughter, and sister-in-law. After my daughters were born and when we moved out of the joint family into our rented apartment, I enjoyed managing the home and taking care of the children. I made lovely clothes for my daughters and supported my husband in his entrepreneurial ventures.

I enjoyed learning, and during the course of my marriage, I kept doing random certifications though I did not use them to actually earn, as it was not encouraged. When my children went to pre-school, my husband was happy to get me a part-time job as an announcer in the local radio station, which was considered a hobby and therefore permitted. In summary, while I broke tradition and married a man of my choosing, in all else I lived up to the expectations of the Indian middle class woman's place in her own household and in society.

It took about ten years for me to finally acknowledge to myself and accept that my marriage was not happy for me. My husband did not have any bad habits and was a loving father. But it started to become very apparent that we were just incompatible in how we approached life, given our different upbringing and family backgrounds—things we were too young and in love to fully understand when we got married but which were now becoming more and more apparent as we brought our daughters into this world and began parenting them. The differences in the outlook between our communities, the dissimilarities in my husband's and my values on numerous little and big things, on how we raised our children and provided for them, on how we lived, our vision for the future, on what we wanted in our lives for our family, and what role we saw both our in-laws playing in that—all of this became material and created significant and sustained daily conflicts: shouting matches, tears, silences, hurt, heartache, all of it.

Feeling helpless to change this situation, I would vent my frustration on my girls. As an example, I would scold them when they returned late on a weekday after visiting their paternal grandparents, which was no fault of theirs. I realized that my daughters were growing up in a dysfunctional home that was creating bad habits for them and for me. It started becoming clearer to me that I wanted my girls, especially as they were girls, to grow up with different values and expectations than the ones they were being raised with—than the ones I had been raised with. I wanted them to have the choices I never had. Again, my husband was a good father and many of my relatives would tell me how I needed to adjust and accept my lot. At least my husband did not cheat on me, did not beat the kids or me, was not an alcoholic, and did not have any terrible habits. At least he loved us. But apparently for me, this love was not enough, not just by itself. There were other equally important things that a marriage needed and good parenthood made mandatory.

As I began thinking about a separation, I realized that if I wanted to raise my girls my way, then I would need to be financially independent and be able to support them. After being unhappy for the last five years of that ten-year marriage, it took me two more years to finally work up the courage and willpower to break societal norms again in a different way and seek a divorce. In the mean time I took courses, learned, found one job, and then the next better paying one. And then I sought and got that divorce and sole custody of my girls.

Divorced, Broke, and Alone

It was the early 1990s and I was 35 by the time my marriage was officially over. I had been awarded custody of our two daughters. During the course of my divorce, I had moved to Bangalore from Chennai, where I had lived all my life until then, on account of my job. My parents took a little time to accept my decision to separate from my husband, the way they took time to accept our union before. However, once they came around, they were kind enough to move in with us to help me care for my daughters in the new city. My brother, who lived in the United States, sent us money every month to support our living expenses. I had been granted divorce under the stipulation that, since I was employed, I did not want anything from my husband to support my daughters and me. At the point of my divorce, I was in my third job in two years and a long way off from making enough money to sustain my family and myself.

I was ashamed and depressed that I wasn't earning enough to manage my family. I felt like a parasite depending on my brother and my parents. I felt rotten that, as an adult and parent, I didn't have the wherewithal to be independent, self-sufficient, and I did not have it together enough to raise my girls on my own.

The road to reach the goal of financial self-sufficiency seemed very long and unending for a home science graduate with basic computer skills. It felt hopeless. There was blame. I blamed my mother for my degree in home science, that she forced me into, while a science degree would have been my choice and would have helped me find a better job sooner in my life. There was anger. I was angry at all the injustice I had suffered in my divorce and children's custody hearings. There was isolation. I felt ostracized by my relatives and society, and some even questioned and implied infidelity to my husband as the reason for my defection. It made me so mad but also sad.

The children struggled too. They had been doing well in school in Chennai and now had to join another school in Bangalore, adapt to a new curriculum, and learn the language of the state. They had to make new friends in school and in the neighborhood. They had accepted the fact that their lives were with me, for the most part. They were old enough to understand the situation—some of it. But it was hard on them as society (the people) and societal systems (the institutions, expectations, processes, etc.) weren't ready for them. I know they dealt with challenges of their own, being daughters of a divorcée in a country that always asked girls, "So what does your father/husband do?"—something they couldn't answer anymore as my husband and I were completely estranged and had no contact after the divorce and custody hearings. There was some shame, some blame, and a lot of adjusting. For something as simple as a signature on a grade report card, they faced questions and comments from teachers and classmates about why their father's signature was not there and why it was their mom's. As I said before, society was not set up to support my girls as daughters of a divorcée and not a two-parent, husband and wife, man/woman household. They heard comments on their personality and development like, "She is like this because she does not have a father." They heard comments on their mother and how she was a bad parent. They heard many things and as a result grew up faster to be adults—faster than they would have as children of a two-parent household.

Socially, I had estranged myself from most of my relatives since my situation was totally outside of the norms of the India of those years. I had married in the later 1970s to a person of my own choice, which was unheard of in the middle class, especially across religious and community boundaries. And then, a dozen years later, I decided that the marriage was not working and worked to end it. Society said, "First she fights to have her way, goes against our advice and marries him and now she is divorced and that is another shocking disgrace to her family! Poor parents!"

My friends were all in Chennai where I grew up, married and living their lives. In those days there was no email, or social media technology to help you stay in touch. There was no time to write letters and no money for long distance calls. I also did not want to keep talking about my situation to different sets of people who would then offer sympathy and advice. I wanted to focus totally on the next steps and recreate my life on my own. And so I was alone in many ways—some of my choosing, and others due to circumstances. And while I was lucky enough to have help in the form of my family, as you can see, dear reader, the road was not easy.

My biggest angst was the question, "Why was I given two amazing children without the means to bring them up?" If there was one dream, one burning desire, it was financial self-sufficiency to pay my rent and bills, buy our daily bread, and pay for the school fees; it was that I get to a place where I could manage it all on my own and do it successfully. In the meantime, my girls and I managed and supported each other and made the best of the tough life we faced.

The Light at the End of the Tunnel

It was my fourth job in an Information Technology services company that gave me the opportunity to stabilize my life financially. I was finally in an environment where I was learning and growing while the company was expanding and the IT industry in India was entering its huge growth spurt. I was in the right place at the right time. Joining as an administrative assistant, I soon moved to the computer infrastructure department, thanks to my thirst for computer knowledge.

In two years, with the company growing rapidly, I had a five-digit Indian salary that was enough for the basic needs of my daughters and myself and to start saving a bit for the children's future. I had attained my goal of financial self-sufficiency! I was exultant! Things started looking up from then on. I bought a condo for our family a few years later.

As my life started rebuilding with some goals achieved such as adequate earning, children growing up with scholastic success, and the ownership of our own home, my relatives acknowledged that my decision to get divorced was the right one and that I was a successful person. My strong financial circumstances, and the way my daughters reflected the values I had tried to instill in them, made many of my relatives praise me for being a good parent and provider. Many had thought I could not do it and most believed that I should not have done what I did. But I needed to be a single mom, creating my own path in life to retain my self-respect. It still took me time to renew my relationships with relatives and friends but it eventually happened. And during this journey, I learned lessons and practiced them to become a stronger person—a better mother—the breadwinner for the family.

My journey from a broke homemaker to a breadwinner took about two years, and my daughters were on their own feet in about ten years from my divorce. I even opted to retire at 60 years old even though I started late, in my thirties. At that point, I wanted to and could embark on a second career that involved supporting other women in their aspirations to independence and self-sufficiency. This had been my passion all along. Already my relatives and friends were referring to me their friends whose marriages were breaking up and suggesting that I offer moral support, guidance, coaching, and mentoring to those women. And I am happy to say that those women were able to piece their lives together and move towards progress for themselves and their children, just like I did. Such rewarding experiences made me choose to be a life coach after my retirement from my IT career and now to talk to you, my readers, through this book.

Chapter 3

MY RECIPE FOR SUCCESS–AN INTRODUCTION TO THE SIX INGREDIENTS

"We are the creative force of our life, and through our own decisions rather than our conditions, if we carefully learn to do certain things, we can accomplish those goals."

—Stephen Covey

During the 10 years of my single mom story, I did not spend any time looking at the past. My brain was filled with only, "What's next?" When I was on the mission of raising my daughters and pursuing a career, I did not have time to reflect on ingredients and principles; one lived and learned. Self-development books sometimes showed the way. It was after I became a life coach in my second career that I found time to dwell upon what helped me fulfill my role as a parent as well as enjoy a satisfying career. It was then that I discovered ingredients and principles that had worked for me.

I had adopted some principles to live my life by and was sharing them with those who asked for my advice. As I shared these ingredients with new Super Single Moms, I kept hearing from them how much these helped them be and feel stronger in facing their challenges, and how they could now approach life with confidence and faith in themselves. Thus the RECIPE for my success was derived from my reflections on what helped me and the other Super Single Moms I mentored as a life coach. My RECIPE was born and it became the idea of this book.

Given that I have been in similar situations as a single mom as you probably are, I thought that these ingredients could be of some use and value to you, my reader. These ingredients helped me commit to the single-mom life I had chosen. They gave me the courage and conviction to stay on course. They guided me when I had to choose between options and they pointed me the right way. They brought me contentment and peace of mind. They miraculously opened doors and paths that I did not know existed and made my mind and heart receptive to the gifts my life brought.

And here I am, ready to share them with you, with the hope that they may be useful and valuable to you also. I hope they provide you the answers to your questions, solve your problem of making it as a single breadwinner mom, and make you feel whole and super. Most of all, I hope you can use these ingredients in your recipe for success too.

This RECIPE is actually the acronym for my 6 ingredients:

R—**R**esponsibility to Your Children
E—**E**arning, Earning Potential, and Money Management
C—The Power of **C**onviction
I—**I**ntentional Learning
P—**P**ersonal Care as Paramount
E—**E**mbracing Your Reality

Below, I introduce you to each of these six ingredients. The next six chapters go into greater depth, laying out the characteristics of each of these six ingredients and how they help.

R—Responsibility to Your Children

You are a Super Single Mom mainly by one qualification: that you are a *mom*. It therefore follows that the most important focus in your life is your children. You have undertaken the major responsibility of bringing them up; they are your highest priority and around them revolves everything you do. You are responsible for them. You take care of their every need, their satisfaction and well-being. They are your most important clients and their satisfaction is key to your happiness. However, in the emotional state you are in, especially after your divorce, you may go through a variety of feelings.

You feel an overwhelming sense of duty to ensure their well being. You feel ownership of them as they are yours (literally a part of you) and you are now taking charge of their lives because you believe you know what is good for them. You worry for them, at times so much so that you are left feeling like their wellbeing is a burden too huge to carry alone. You feel pride in their accomplishments because they are yours and you have a stake in their life and it feels like their accomplishments are yours. Your children are your anchor, your reason for waking up in the morning, and your reason for sleepless nights. They are your source of joy and the bane of your existence at the same time.

How can you be responsible *to* them while also being responsible *for* them? The way I learned to look after my children was to be their guardian-mom. I do not mean guardian in the legal sense of the term. However, as their guardian mom, if you start to see yourself as more their caretaker and less as their mother to whom they belong, you will find that your relationship with them will strengthen tremendously. When you stop treating them as *yours*, your unconscious and at times selfish ownership of them reduces and you begin to notice and let go of all the positive and negative emotions, thoughts, and actions that come with it. Instead, you start seeing them as your clients—as children of the world who need you to serve them and care for them.

As the caretaker of my children, I had to carefully bring them up with my best efforts as they were not mine but were under my charge. I also had to release them into the world as adults and not hold on to them. Making this as a conscious commitment to them—that my responsibility to them was as their guardian-mom—is the first ingredient that was the basis of my single-mom life, and it paid off in ways beyond my imagination. More on this in Chapter 4.

E—Earning, Earning Potential, and Money Management

If children are your clients, money is one of the most tangible resources that help satisfy your needs and caters to your ability to serve them. Not having enough of it is your greatest angst and having enough of it enables you to care for your family. While money alone can't buy happiness, it is important that you as a single mom have the ability to earn to provide. Money helps you avoid dependency on others.

After being a broke homemaker, believing in and enhancing your own earning potential is very much needed. And yet, this is often the hardest step—getting over your own feelings of inadequacy and lack and forging ahead in the job market.

And as earning does not happen in a vacuum, you will also read about strengthening your relationship with money and wealth through money management.

As the breadwinner single mom, you need a vocation to earn for your family and also to have a purposeful and productive life for yourself. Earning offers a sense of accomplishment even as it offers you an opportunity to create and live an identity as someone other than a mom.

In Chapter 5, I will share with you my approach to earning, earning potential, and money management. This second ingredient is about earning for yourself and your family and doing it in a way that matters.

C—The Power of Conviction

In my life, faith played a very important role in my ability to change myself from a homemaker to a breadwinner single mom. It made me courageous, confident, calm, and centered and opened paths that I didn't know existed. Faith in God, or the Universe, or just being positive, draws good things to you. This means you think, feel, and act based on positive energy, with purpose, passion, and conviction. So I would like to share with you this ingredient of having faith in Chapter 6.

I—Intentional Learning

In your journey of the single mom from homemaker to breadwinner and beyond, life gives you plenty of opportunities to learn and grow. Aside from formal education that you may undertake to enhance your earning power, learning from life experiences is also equally valuable. To benefit from the lessons of life, you need to be open and receptive to learning from them. You need to become an *intentional learner*, who looks for learning opportunities in everything you are going through. Learning with intent helps you free yourself from obsolete baggage from the past and enriches your new life as a single mom with meaningful and relevant new ideas and guidance. Eliminating the need for perfection and accepting that you will make mistakes, you can learn, unlearn, or relearn what matters. Your journey as a single mom will thus be progressive and richer than what you can imagine. Chapter 7 lays out in more detail this key ingredient.

P—Personal Care is Paramount

Chapter 8 is about self-care. While caring for the family is of the utmost priority, caring for the self is what will sustain us. Within all the constraints and challenges of being a single mom, you can and should find ways of caring for yourself. When you feel you have had adequate quantity and quality of time for yourself, you can ward off self-pity, fatigue, anger, and a plethora of other negative emotions that get in the way of playing your role very well. I cannot stress enough the importance of this ingredient.

E—Embracing Your Reality

The last ingredient (Chapter 9) is almost the sum total of all the previous ones, like the whole picture versus its component pieces in a jigsaw puzzle. It is taking full charge and responsibility for your life and what it entails as a single mom, without the emotional encumbrances of guilt, regret, self-pity, and anger. It means letting go of baggage that no longer serves you, and looking at your life in all the various roles that you have to play, including motherhood. You get to understand that your journey as a single mom will take enormous sustained effort and you have to be prepared to gear up your physical, mental, and spiritual energies to make it both successful and enjoyable. You will also know that your role as a single mom empowers you to have the authority and responsibility to make choices that sometimes make sense to you alone. This is what embracing your reality is all about.

In the final chapter in this book (Chapter 10) I also share with you some of the blocks that can get in the way of progress in your life as a single mom. It is important to become aware of them and understand that you might need help to overcome them. Recognizing your blocks is often the biggest challenge all human beings face and as a single mom you are no different. We all have thoughts and emotions that sometimes get in the way of us living our life to the fullest. So this chapter introduces you to some of them so that you can begin to know and understand how they play out in your life.

What is not included in my book is information on how to have the next love in your life. When my marriage fell apart, there was no other purpose in my life than to earn and provide for my children. There was no time or interest in pursuing another union. While many single moms find their lives blessed with a second and happier marriage or partnership, the focus of my book is on functioning as an independent adult and finding fulfillment within yourself.

Making This RECIPE Work for You

I write this book and share my RECIPE with you in the hope that it helps you realize your goals for your single-mom life. I hope the six ingredients form the potion that makes your wishes, hopes, and dreams for your life come true. You will read in much more detail in the next chapters also how the six ingredients helped me and other single moms.

I offer examples from my life and the lives of some of my single mom clients. You will learn from them what each ingredient signifies, how each played—and continues to play—a significant role in our journeys as single moms. I will share with you the problems that these ingredients helped address and how each one helped us move forward. You will begin to recognize them, understand their purpose, and know the way to practice them so that these ingredients become your own recipe for success.

At the end of each of these chapters, I have summarized for you the main messages in the chapter and have offered some questions for you to ponder over so that you can find what ingredients are missing in your life as a single mom and where you can incorporate them to be better and stronger.

Read on now to understand how the ingredients can be used to create your RECIPE for success!

INGREDIENT 1–RESPONSIBILITY TO YOUR CHILDREN

"It is not what you do for your children, but what you have taught them to do for themselves, that will make them successful human beings."

—Ann Landers

When pregnant mothers are asked what they enjoy the most about their pregnancy, they unequivocally answer that feeling the movement of the baby inside them makes all the other discomforts of pregnancy fade away. After having life inside you for nine months, having the baby in your arms is one of the most wondrous moments of motherhood. And, as a mom, you often pin all your hopes and dreams on your little bundle of joy.

Whether they are planned or whether they just happened (as in my case) you consciously or unconsciously have many wishes for your children. You want to give them everything good you have experienced and you want to give them things you yourself could not have as a child.

Material things. Values. Habits. Behaviors. Everything! You want your children to excel in academics, extracurricular activities, and sports. You dream of them earning well and becoming famous in their professions. You want them to listen to you, love you, and respect you, and you think and believe that you know what is best for them. You want them to grow up to think that they had the best, most rocking mom in the whole world. You feel proud of their accomplishments and you project all your wishes and desires for them onto them. Most importantly, you share and nurture these dreams and aspirations in partnership with your spouse.

Then one day, you become a single mom and now that picture that you had painted as a couple is a vision you are striving towards alone. What is hard is reconciling the fact that the shared vision for your children's future may now be impossible because you don't know if you can do it alone. You want to, but you are not sure it is possible, given that you are now a single parent and just trying to survive. You are starting from scratch. You have to provide for their life and your own, alone. How can you give them everything you thought they needed and everything you had hoped and dreamed for them?

On the one hand, the fact that you have the children in your legal custody must be of great relief to you because you can influence their lives in the right ways. The instability of a rocky marriage and the trials and tribulations of the separation or divorce are behind you. But as a breadwinner starting late, it is overwhelming to provide for all their needs—a safe home, education, health, all the opportunities for them to realize their potential, and certainly not the least, love and care. And as a result, at times, your frustration with other things—stress, exhaustion, lack of sleep, worry, hunger, anxiety, work, or just taking care of day-to-day things—could show up in your interactions with them. At the end of your day, when you are tired, you may not have the energy to deal with their squabbles or stubbornness. You want them to feel no lack of opportunities and as you toil, struggle, and work hard to provide for their material needs from daybreak to dusk, sometimes they get the short end of the stick.

You want them to do things your way because you want to ensure that your dreams for them become a reality and you feel the pressure of ensuring this tenfold as a single parent. You want them to succeed spectacularly because their success means that you are a success as a mom. And that is important to you right now because being a mom is your biggest identity at this time. You think you failed in your role as a wife as you are now divorced; and you are very insecure about your identity as a breadwinner as you are new to this role. So in your own mind it becomes imperative that you succeed in your role as a single-mom. So much pressure! And the children face the brunt of this pressure sometimes.

Notwithstanding your emotional state, you have to think of your children's too. Children love both their parents. They may not understand why their parents are not living together, why they are not with both their parents all the time. They will throw tantrums, ask for their father, and declare why they like their father more than they do you (at that moment). How do you handle their resistance, anger, or negativity? You are worried about paying off the bills and making ends meet and in the middle of all that you have to coddle and cajole your children! And you ask yourself: "How can I still be the best mom in middle of everything else?" I will share with you what helped me in my life.

The Birth of the Guardian-Mom Philosophy

It was the summer of 1992. I was in between jobs 3 and 4. As you know, my parents lived with me and helped take care of my children, who were 13 and 11 years old. My brother sent us money every month for our expenses.

I have said this before but in all my life, that was the darkest time. I was dejected that I was 36 and still dependent on others for my life, desperate for a job opening, and depressed that the next job was nowhere in sight. I lamented why I was given two children when I was not given the means to raise them. I was judging myself as a mom and breadwinner and found myself completely lacking in every way. How could I be a good mom to them when all I wanted to do was sleep all day to shut out the hopelessness and despondency of my situation?

It was during this low period in my life that I came across something in the Readers' Digest magazine that my parents subscribed to, under the section Quotable Quotes. I don't remember the exact words but it said something like: "Your children are not yours as you think; they are just God's way of perpetuating life on earth." These were profound words for me. I felt a huge sense of awakening when I read those words—a light going on in my head. I thought, "My children are God's and my role is that of God's delegate guardian. All I have to do is to do my best for these children of God." Those words reverberated in my head for many days and I tried to make sense of them—what they meant to me in my role as a single mom. It is from these thoughts that I derived my guardian-mom philosophy. I share with you below the insights I was left with as to what it meant for me to be in this new role. It meant:

- The universe/God deemed that I was good enough to be the conduit for bringing God's children as my daughters on planet earth. That was why I was their mother.
- As such, I have been vested with the responsibility of raising them to adulthood. I am accountable to the universe for doing my best for these children.
- My mission is to raise them as their caretaker. And since this role is transient, I can't be attached to my children. But I have to put in my most sincere effort in raising them.

- Since they are God's children, and I am their assigned caretaker, it is my responsibility and duty to raise them to be good citizens of the universe.
- These children have their own unique contributions to offer to the world.
- I have to nourish and make sure their unique identities and strengths are developed so that they are enabled to light up the world.

This deep realization, this central understanding, and all of the above insights made me clear about *why* I had these two children and *what* my mission was. I was filled with renewed strength and purpose and unconsciously started reformulating my expectations for both myself as a single mom and for my girls. I now saw myself, not as a perfect/ imperfect mother or a good /bad mom, but as a caretaker guardian-mom who had to sincerely try her best to do what was right for her girls.

What Does it Mean to be a Guardian-Mom?

My new perspective on what motherhood and parenting entailed now as a guardian-mom is as follows:

- As a mom, I felt *ownership* towards my children; that meant I was free to treat them as I thought fit. Now as their guardian-mom, I felt *responsibility* to nourish and cherish them, as they deserved, irrespective of my personal moods and feelings; I had to serve them as best as I could.
- As a parent, I would feel pride in their achievements, because they were *my* children; as their guardian mom, I encouraged them to achieve for their own satisfaction; *I was just happy for their joy in their achievements.*

- I wanted them to achieve great material success because their success reflected my success as their mother; but as their guardian-mom, I desired that they be good global citizens who would make a positive difference in the world and be successful for the world and not for my motherhood to be deemed a success.
- As a parent, I wanted them to listen to what I said and obey me; in my guardian-mom role, I had to listen and open my mind and heart to the truth in what they said.
- As a mom, I imposed my dreams on them, while as a guardian-mom, I understood that they had the right to their own dreams.
- I worried about them as a mom; in my guardian-mom role, I felt grateful for their well-being and encouraged them if they took thoughtful risks.
- When I loved them as a mom, I thought they had to respect me; when I thought I was their guardian-mom, I respected and appreciated them for loving me.
- I would have always been their mom; but after my guardianship, I also had them as my younger friends.

Do you understand the difference? Shifting your traditional mom role and orientation into that of a guardian-mom means that you have to be responsible *to* your children as their guardian even as you are responsible *for* them.

Being the Best Guardian-Mom

So I told you about my guardian-mom philosophy. What does it look like in real life? How do you manifest it? How should you think, feel, and act in order to be the best guardian-mom? Even for me, practicing this philosophy took conscious effort. Many times in my single-mom life I was naturally the mom, but then had to remind myself of my role as guardian-mom that then guided me in the right way to respond to my children. To help you further understand what the responsibility of raising your children looks like when you are a guardian-mom, I offer you five principles that I adopted. I hope these principles can help you internalize the guardian-mom philosophy in your life, as they did in my clients' lives and mine. The five principles are as follows:

- Bring up your children to be adults; teach them to fish and don't just hand over fish to them
- Love your children unconditionally and without strings attached
- Let go when it is time
- Do your best without guilt over what you can't do for your children; let them achieve on their own what you couldn't give them
- Practice open, honest, compassionate communication

Now, you must have heard these ideas before. They are out there and have been for a long time. But they have a special relevance here in the execution of my guardian-mom philosophy. So let me go into a little more detail explaining these.

As a guardian-mom, bring up your children to be adults; teach them to fish and don't just hand over fish to them

Human beings have the most helpless young ones among all life. Our babies need to be fed, clothed, and cleaned up for the first few *years* of life. Then we teach our children to eat and dress by themselves. By the time they are ready to go to pre-school, they are nearly physically independent. But what usually happens is that, instead of further developing that independence, we can't stop doing things for them. We have gotten so used to thinking and caring for them and their needs (because we knew their needs before they could even express their needs as babies) that we can't stop. We continue to impose on them our habit of thinking for them, assuming we know what is best, as we have, all these years. So we continue to make their beds, pack their lunches, remind them of their homework, wake them up to go to school; as a result, both the children and the parents get habituated to having the parents do for the children what they can be taught to do for themselves. This gets perpetuated in other areas as well. We dismiss children's thoughts, opinions, and feelings as transient because "they don't understand." We think for them. Act for them. Dream for them. And make decisions for them. Remember how you started your parenthood with hopes, dreams, and expectations of and for your children as their mom? Well, all of that comes in the way of allowing the mental and emotional freedom for your children to dream their own dreams and pursue their own aspirations. It blocks their natural tendencies of becoming independent, and can create laziness and complacency in them and a habit of abdicating their responsibilities as adults.

So teaching them to fish and not just handing over fish to them means that you raise children to become adults in the true sense of adulthood. You raise them to be physically, mentally, emotionally, and financially independent. There is no different goal for boys and girls. Every single child needs to be taught to become an independent adult—to be able to live on their own, physically and financially, to take ownership of their thoughts, feelings, and actions; to be able to make choices and learn from their occasional failures. You will then fulfill your responsibility of raising them to be good citizens of the universe—adults who can then take on their share of responsibility to the world.

In practical terms, it would mean all young adults should know the basics of making their own food, keeping their environment clean, and earning enough to pay for their separate dwelling, clothes, and transport. They need to understand the power of choice and the consequences of decision-making. And it does not matter if after attaining adulthood they choose to live with somebody else or not.

So how do you teach fishing and not give them fish? I am sure there are a lot of great books and information on children's milestones and the behaviors expected at each of those. But many times, you let yourself succumb to expediency and your own standards of efficiency and don't give your children enough time to practice being independent. Your child's room is untidy, you want him or her to clean it up, and that is the rule. But when you are expecting visitors, you think of your standard of cleanliness and how your guests might think badly of your mothering ability at seeing the dirty room, so you tidy up your child's room yourself because, despite numerous times being told, you child hasn't. As a result, you contribute to your child's laziness and increase the habit for his/her dependency on you to do his/her chores.

Remember, as a guardian-mom the issue is not that they are not listening to you when they do not clean their room. The issue is that they learn how to clean their room and take ownership of it. It is important that you teach them gently and slowly how to be independent by making sure they clean their room rather than you doing it for them.

Similarly, you may be contributing to your child's lack of independence and self-sufficiency in the name and guise of love and care. It goes something like this: "Oh poor thing, let me just do this one thing for them, they must be tired or upset." Or it could be frustration and you being fed up that leads to you doing things for your children—things they can do on their own if push comes to shove; if they had to sink or swim. So do not enable or create dependency where there doesn't need to be one, due to your own conscious or unconscious thoughts and feelings or societal pressures. Reflecting on your own behavior will give you answers about the barriers that are coming in the way of you raising your children to learn to fish rather than just eat the fish you give them.

So the most important point here is to avoid standing in the way of the child's own independent tendencies as well as to give the child time to practice independence in a safe way.

Based on this principle, my client Lakshmi's rule for her daughters Sweta and Sita was: "Study whatever you are interested in, but at 25 (in India parents pay for their children's education till post-graduation which could take up to 25 years to complete), you will be expected to earn for yourself. And if you happen to live with me, you will have to pay for your bed and board." She did not stipulate how much they had to earn; she just said that if they had expensive tastes, they should make sure their income would pay for them. For Lakshmi, this was her way of fostering independence and adulthood for her daughters. As her daughters grew up, Sweta did pay for her rent and food while she lived in Lakshmi's home for a few years when she had her first job. Sita lived and worked in another city after her university, so she too was independent at 25. Though Lakshmi did not need her daughters' money, it was the principle that they all honored. This financial independence would give her daughters the confidence to fend for themselves in the world—something Lakshmi never had as she had never earned before her divorce.

Of course, there are situations where the children are challenged in some way. But I truly believe that all children can be taught to become independent to the extent they can. The goal should be to make them full-fledged adults and the efforts should be in that direction. When I was young, we used to buy UNICEF greetings cards for New Years and I used to be amazed at the foot and mouth paintings by artists on those cards! Imagine the sense of self-worth differently-abled children can develop when they are encouraged to become self-sufficient! So don't have low expectations for any of your children based on the labels you have or society has imposed on them because they are differently abled or are not living up to the expectations of others. Help them be the most independent they can be. Never feel sorry for them or angry with them for not living up to your expectations. Your job is putting in the effort and time with patience, kindness, respect, and love for the child.

A final example of teaching your children to fish vs. feeding them fish is allowing them to make choices and decisions. It has to be about them choosing their path rather than you imposing your path "for their well-being" on them. Let them choose their career, let them put in the effort to figure out what they want to do and what they would be good at to take on as a career. Don't give them fish by telling them what degree they should pursue or who they should marry. Share with them your concerns or suggestions and ask them questions that will help them think through their decisions. So teach them how to fish.

To reiterate, teaching your children to fish is not about them obeying your orders because you know that it is good for them to be independent. It is about you giving them the tools to be self-sufficient adults and treating them respectfully as they grow into one. It is about you helping them understand why this is important, teaching them how to get there, and them figuring out what they want to be. They do not "owe it to you" to do something or be something. So help them see that you are teaching them to fish. And help your clients (i.e., your children) understand that they no longer need your services as their "mom."

And what is the reward for teaching your children to fish? Your children become expert fishermen and women and sometimes even feed you fish that they have caught so you get some rest! Got my point?

As a guardian-mom, love your children unconditionally and without strings attached

As a parent you will have expectations for your children and you also impose your expectations on them. You are sacrificing so much for them, you are working so hard to give them a good life, so is it too much to expect them to understand your reasoning behind decisions, your rationale for your choices? But even young children have their own preferences and likes and dislikes. Their feelings are real to them (and to you, especially when they feel negatively about you). Conflicts may arise and in such situations, your love for them gets submerged under the clash of egos and your children just want to lash out at you because they are hurting.

Here is where the principle of loving unconditionally and showing that love helps. What does this mean? It means that you, as the older person, the adult, are emotionally strong and accept your children's negative emotions, acknowledge them, and say that you understand them. You get past your own hurt and open your head and heart to what your children are feeling and saying. You are patient and you discuss solutions with them in a way they can understand.

One important commitment I made to my daughters when I had to be their leader in life was that they could choose to live with their father once they were 18 and old enough. I told them as the marriage was breaking up and I had to take charge of them, "Right now you guys need a single leader and that's me for various reasons; if at 18, you think that you want to be with your father, I would not mind at all. I will always love you and be there for you when you need me." I don't know if they really understood what I was saying at that time but I stated this many times to them and I meant it. My 18-year rule was created by my insecurity and fear of my ex-husband disrupting our lives.

It was a few years later that I discovered that my younger daughter Divya had been in touch with her dad a few years after our separation. She would call him and talk to him periodically. When I came to know about it I was upset with her, wondering if I was not enough as a parent for her. I was angry with her for disobeying my request. But I soon realized that if I could accept her choosing to be with her dad at 18, I could accept that she wanted to be in touch with him right now. Her love for him did not mean that she did not love me. I remembered my guardian-mom philosophy. So I told her that it was fine by me and that I understood her need to be connected to him. I encouraged her to continue keeping in touch with him and asked her if I could facilitate that in any other way.

While Divya did have her loyalty towards her father, she also later told me that raising us as a single mom was the best decision for all of us and that she and her sister got the best for their lives under my parenthood. In some of my clients' lives, they have had the reverse situation of having to surrender the children's custody to their father; later on, the children connected back with their mothers as adults and understood the circumstances of their separation. It is up to us, as single moms, to be emotionally strong to let our children love other people who may not be our choices to love, without feeling rejected or let down. It's about your love giving space and the freedom to your children to return it, instead of binding them with it.

In the India where I grew up, it is very common that parents subject their adult children to emotional blackmail in order to make the children behave as the parents want them to and accept the parents' decisions and choices. "If you married a person outside of our community, then we will not be your parents anymore; we will sever ties with you," was a very common cliché. What you are hearing is the condition for love and approval from the parents. This is all so unnecessary. Loving your children unconditionally means that you give your inputs to your children, then accept their decisions and support their life forward in whatever way you can.

My client Lakshmi stressed to her daughters that they would need to make decisions themselves as adults. This was put to the test when Sweta and Sita were finishing school and had to figure out what they wanted to major in, in college. Lakshmi's hope was that at least one of her daughters, if not both, should be an information technology professional. She nudged Sweta and Sita into taking the special classes that would help them secure places in IT under-grad courses. But neither of them was interested in IT. Sweta chose to study commerce and Sita favored communications. As Lakshmi started getting more and more upset about their decisions and arguments ensued, I reminded Lakshmi about the guardian-mom approach. Through coaching she realized that her loving them and paying for their education did not mean they had to do what she wanted them to do. While she may want to make decisions for her daughters, it was their life and they had to live it. After all, they couldn't take ownership of their lives if they did not have a hand in deciding what it was going to be. So Lakshmi acknowledged her problem, apologized to her daughters, gracefully gave in to their wishes, and supported them in their choices for their future. Remember that loving unconditionally means that you no longer expect your children to fall in line with all your wishes, that you can live with their choices without throwing a tantrum about it.

As a guardian-mom, let go when it is time

Your role as a guardian-mom also means that there is an end date to it. You can choose when that date will be or it can just happen circumstantially. Having that end date does not mean that you are not available to your children as their guardian-mom anymore. It just means that you are taking a step back, letting them live their lives, and are now focusing on your life as something other than being their mom.

All through their lives, your children will develop their own opinions, and make their own decisions, regardless of what you think they should do. In fact, you—as a parent—need to keep nudging them into becoming independent in every way. It is the goal of becoming an adult not just chronologically and legally, but in the true sense we saw earlier. And once they have reached a point where they are ready, you have to let them go. Like a doctor who is a good one if his/her patients are completely cured and don't have to come back to him/her, your goal is to raise them to let them soar. And you have to let them go for them to soar. You have to remember this all through your journey as a single mom.

Letting go is the process of detaching yourself from their immediate lives, if and when the situation demands it. Just like you are propelling your child towards adulthood and independence, you have to prepare to sideline yourself from their daily lives as they become adults. You have to get ready when you are no longer the most important person in their lives, when they cut your telephone call saying, "Mom, I'm busy, I'll call later," without feeling a sense of loss. You have to accept and respect that they are capable and ready to make their own choices without consulting you. You have to make sure that you have replaced the time you spent on caring for them with other purposeful and fulfilling activities so that their physical absence is not creating a huge void in your life. You have to shed the worry of whether they are following all your self-care rules and your advice on various things. This is the time when you should feel happy that you have done your share of their growing up (very well, I should say!) and now can rest a little bit.

Indian parents are famous for fondly telling their children, "Whatever age you are, you will always be my child, so…" The "so" is usually followed by a parent demand or command. What is often implied here is parental expectation and control disguised as love. If you have taught your fishing lessons for your children well and love your children without any strings attached, letting go should be an easy and natural phenomenon.

But as a single mom, you can get bogged down by normal human feelings—of pride at your children's accomplishments, disappointment or anger at their choices, hurt when they don't reciprocate your sentiments, and so on. Your children provided you with the motivation to progress in your life, to make it on your own, but this can also lead to your not having any other purpose in life. Your whole world can center on them and later you don't know how to separate yourself from being your children's mom.

Preeti was my client and her daughter Meena, during her undergrad years, wanted to live closer to her college. She wanted to be in the student leadership body and eventually run for president of the college student government. Their home was quite a distance away from her college and the commute both ways would take a long time, given the traffic in the city they lived. It was not a normal Indian living arrangement for a young woman to live separately before her marriage when her family was in the same city. Preeti had just bought her first home with a room furnished to suit her daughter's tastes. Imagine her disappointment that Meena wanted to be away from the family. But Preeti understood Meena's goals, ambitions, and her desire to serve in the student union. With coaching she realized she had to let go so that Meena could soar. Fortunately, Preeti could also afford paying for the extra rooming her daughter needed. So Preeti fully supported her in her move. Meena did later become president of her college student government. While it was hard not to feel protective about her daughter, Preeti exercised the guardian-mom rule and let her young one fly away from the nest when she was ready for it. While the house felt empty without her daughter, Preeti enrolled for some glass painting classes and enjoyed her free evenings doing some reading and watching television. She looked forward to the weekends when she got to spend time with Meena when she visited. It made them closer as mother-daughter. As you can see, Preeti was able to let go and move on to the next chapter in her life.

So, dear single mom, remember and practice your guardian-mom role—it involves being responsible and loving, in a detached way. It means that your job is over at some point and you need to let your children take charge of their lives. It means not imposing your will and your desires on them. It means you teach them universal values and inculcate in them the ability to distinguish right from wrong. How they use these in making their decisions is left to them. When you do this, you will actually feel relieved when they become adults and no longer depend on you for everything. Most importantly, letting go will bring your children back to you as young adults seeking your mentorship and friendship. What more could a parent ask for?

As a guardian-mom, do your best without guilt at what you can't do for your children; let them achieve on their own what you couldn't give them

As a single mom, you want to give everything that your children want; you are toiling for what you think they need and what they think they want. You feel guilty sometimes that you can't afford the things they want. It could be the school choice or extracurricular lessons or holidays; there are constraints that you can't overcome.

There is no rule in life that says that in order to qualify as a Super Single Mom, you have to provide everything that you or your child wants. All that you have to do is your best and explain the constraints. Everybody has grievances against their parents, that something was done or not done. The children of the wealthiest of parents will have complaints of their parents depriving them of something or the other. So will your children have; it is normal. What you can't provide to them as children, they can get for themselves as adults, if the desire for it still remains—and that is what you have to explain to them.

When my daughters were both in their teens, one of their friends went abroad for a holiday with her parents. Almost all my daughters' friends did some form of vacation and I could not afford to offer my daughters any vacation—maybe a local spot for a day's outing (again, maybe!) but nothing out of town and definitely not abroad. They stayed home as I worked. Vacation days were kept for emergencies. Not that my girls complained but I felt the lack. I was earning enough to make ends meet but I could not afford more. So I felt inadequate as a mom.

My brother visited me then and I shared with him how bad I felt. My brother said, "They can take as many vacations as they want and holidays abroad as they want to, when they are old enough and earning for themselves. What you are giving them is more important and more fundamental—the foundation for their future capacity to earn." I was reminded that I was putting in my best effort to meet their needs and how the universe needed them to be raised. The idea of giving them a holiday at this point in our lives was more a want than a need. I realized the difference between needs and wish lists and what my responsibility really was towards my children. I reassessed my feelings and re-aligned myself to my guardian-mom principles. I stopped feeling guilty for what I could not provide and made sure I gave them everything that was important—values, emotional support, willingness to communicate, and listening to them.

Similarly, my client Vidya's son Adi was finishing school and was to go to college for his undergrad. In India, the premier institutes are also very expensive and Vidya knew she could not afford them. She was working a full-time job and even with all her savings she would not be able to afford the tuition for tier-one colleges in India. She would have to borrow money to afford it. Vidya had been talking to Adi about his choice of college and how it would impact them financially. But Adi understood the family's financial constraints and, as a result, despite qualifying and gaining entrance into a tier-one college, because they did not offer any scholarships or tuition waivers, he decided to join one from the next tier of colleges. He did not want his mother to borrow money for his education. He was confident that he would do well enough to be able to start earning when he finished his education. This eased Vidya's worry and guilt. Her ability to communicate with Adi was important and his understanding helped them move forward as a family. As you can see, there is no need for self-flagellation. Celebrate what you are able to provide and feel satisfied with all your efforts.

As a guardian-mom, practice open, honest, compassionate communication

In each of the above four principles, communication plays a very important role. When you are teaching your children to fish, explain to them why learning to fish is important. Share with them the values of independence, of becoming a true adult. Express your unconditional love without letting your ego get in the way. When you make mistakes, admit them and apologize to your children. Confess to your children about your vulnerability in letting go. Explain to them your constraints in providing some of the things that they or you want. While sometimes they may not accept your explanations, as they get older, they can understand the realities of life and grasp your limitations.

Similarly, keep the channels of communication open for them to talk to you about their mistakes, their failures, and their learning. Recognize that their feelings are real for them and empathize with them. Make them feel that you are open for them to share anything in their lives without casting a judgment on them. Let me also throw in a final question: How did you like it when *you* were growing up, your parents' choices for you, their rules, conditions, and explanations, their abilities and limitations in providing you what you wanted? Now it is your turn to be parent and a single one at that. Put yourself in your children's shoes and talk to them with an open heart.

Communication is the key that links everything. Strengthen your relationship with your children as a guardian-mom with this honest, loving, and thoughtful communication.

Chapter Conclusion

I have said a lot about being a guardian-mom and the ways you can be one. But how does it really help you and why is it important? After all, how many two-parent families think of such things? Children happen and the parents bring them up. If you had been from the normal two-parent family, you probably wouldn't even be reading this book! But you, as a single mom, have assumed the role and responsibility of a single parent to your children, and you want to know how this journey can be the best for you and your children.

When I started practicing being a guardian-mom, my expectations for and from my children changed. My treatment of them, my communication with them, and my desires for them changed. Embedding the guardian-mom philosophy helps you sleep better at night because the days then become less guilt-ridden and more conflict-free. It helps you run a happy household since you choose the right responses for your children's demands. It makes your struggles worthwhile because there is no self-blame or imposition associated with your efforts.

Being a guardian-mom means that you are not tied to the outcomes of your efforts. You can enjoy the journey and do not have to wait to reach the destination to do so. You are committed to doing the best you can, as that is your job and you serve your children rather than owning them, as we sometimes unconsciously do as their parent. Being a guardian-mom means being their caregiver/caretaker. You are nurturing them like you would nurture a plant and letting them grow—without a feeling of ownership or expectations that revolve around, "This is my plant so it had better behave this way." From a relationship standpoint, you then put in enormous effort to ensure that they like you as their caretaker.

You do not have all the power to make or break their lives. Imagine letting go of that burden and that huge sense of responsibility that is sometimes so crippling. You are responsible for their well-being and for raising them to be good citizens of the world, but you can't make them perfect. They are not yours to perfect. You have a hand (one of many) in shaping them and you can be an example and help them become the best version of themselves they can be. And when your children are adults and on their own, you are happy to be on the sidelines and also to put up your feet to rest and relax.

Seeing yourself as a guardian-mom is one of the most important ingredients/principles in the RECIPE as you trust yourself and you work every day to earn and maintain their trust in you. How wonderful is that feeling where you can enjoy being a lone parent even as you now struggle to be a first time breadwinner!

Summary

We started this chapter asking how you, as a single mom, are going to accomplish all your dreams and wishes for your children. Understand that the answer to the question of how to give all the things you want for your children is that they are all *your* dreams. What you really need to do is let your child dream and then help him or her live it. Let them fly high. Be the wind beneath their wings as the song goes.

To round up the messages in this chapter,

- Be the best guardian-mom for your children that you can. This means:
- Bring up your children to be independent adults; teach them to fish and don't hand over fish to them.
- Love your children unconditionally and without strings attached.
- Let go when it is time.
- Do your best (without guilt at what you can't do) for your children; let them achieve on their own what you couldn't give them.
- And through it all engage in open, positive, empathetic communication.

Questions for You

- Think of one example of how you can live your life as a guardian-mom.
- What can you teach your children that will enable them to help themselves?
- What are some of the conditions you have based your love for your children on?
- How can you get free of them and show your children that you are free of them?
- What situations regarding your children make you feel guilty? How can you think differently to let go of the guilt?
- Imagine an open and loving conversation with your child. How is the interaction now different?

Chapter 5

INGREDIENT 2—EARNING, EARNING POTENTIAL, AND MONEY MANAGEMENT

"Money will come when you are doing the right thing."
—Mike Phillips

Money is one the most important resources in our lives. Financial independence gives us the ability to live our lives as we see fit without having to answer to others. It is also the precursor to other forms of independence such as choosing where we live, our life style choices, our ability to cater to our needs and wants, etc.

You, the single mom, have just stepped into the reality of earning and being the money provider for yourself and your children. Having been a homemaker all your life and having to now find a job or some means to earn, you are filled with dread. Do you have employable skills? Where will you find a job that pays you your starting salary? How much do you need to support yourself and your children? What expenses can you compromise on? Do you need more than one job?

Who will take care of your children when you work? If the work takes up long hours, how can you spend time with your children? How will you balance it all?

For you, my reader, earning is not just the solution to your immediate monetary needs for your family. In your case, earning is also for your own future, beyond providing for your children. You will hope and do your best to help your children stand on their own feet but remember that you will have to let go of them sometime. At this point, you can't reverse roles and begin to be dependent on them financially. After preparing them for their adult life, you want to continue to be self-sufficient. You want money for rainy days; you want savings for your old age medical and living expenses. Given your experience of being a broke homemaker, you probably, like me, never want to get back to a state where you are fully dependent financially on someone else. You want to have money of your own and, if not that, at least the confidence that you have the capability to earn and should the need ever arise you don't have to depend on anyone else ever again.

A further need that you might fulfill by earning is having a career—a profession that you can identify yourself with—to belong to and contribute to. Having a late beginning, how do you satisfy all these needs and requirements?

On reviewing my life's journey, I can see three distinct phases in my financial status in my life as a single mom: in phase 1, I was finding jobs to just start earning, and the clear goal was financial self-sufficiency. Once I was there, phase 2 was fulfilling my wish list, having enough for my wants, and saving for our future. In phase 3, my children were adults and independent, so I had surplus to help others. I will share with you five principles that helped me during the first two phases of my life. Based on my coaching, I believe these will be the most relevant to you as you begin your journey from broke homemaker to single breadwinner mom.

1—Start Where You Are

I was very late in beginning to earn; I was 33 when I had to find a job to survive. As far as earning went, my starting point was this: I had my radio announcement part-time job but it would not pay remotely enough to support my girls nor myself. I could sew children's clothes and I made beautiful dresses for my daughters, but I lacked the business acumen to make it a living for myself. I had a home science degree and could cook well. These were the qualifications I had as far as my potential to earn went.

I had to start somewhere. So I took the first job I was offered, which was as a sales assistant in a computer hardware firm. I was not picky. I was just grateful that someone even offered me a job. My advice to you, my dear reader, is to just start where you are. Start with something; start somewhere—anywhere, really—that helps you bring in some money. The time for feeling regret, guilt, inadequacy is over and action is needed! So go jump into the pool and learn to swim!

My client Vidya had a bachelor's degree in arts. She got her first job via a friend in a small educational institute as an administrative assistant with a really small salary. But for her, it was a lucky break and she was elated about it. From there she moved ahead in a few years' time. We will talk about that in a bit.

2—Change Jobs as Needed

You will feel good once you begin earning. As you learn the ropes of your job you will gain confidence in your capability to earn. Thereafter, you can make jumps into better paying jobs that align with your interests, or your interests will develop and you can start building your career.

While you are struggling to reach the goal of monetary self-sufficiency, don't be afraid to switch to jobs that offer better pay and benefits, taking care to balance them with your other priorities, such as time with your children and caring for them. Don't let the fact that you started late and have to single-handedly care for your children make you think you deserve to earn less. Initially everything seems hard, but children grow older, and you get more experience at work, so you can and should look forward to attaining your goal of self-sufficiency sooner rather than later.

I moved through three jobs in a span of one and a half years due to reasons within and outside my control. My salary went up from job 1 to job 2 and then remained the same. It was in my fourth job that I finally got into the Human Resources department of an up and coming IT services company with my unimpressive resumé and got a job as an administrative assistant. The salary was still the same as what I had been getting in my previous job, but the company seemed to vibe with positive energy and the people I met were nice.

The company was doing well and the software industry in India was in its boom period, so in a couple of years, I attained my goal of being financially independent. I could pay the rent and the utility bills for my home, pay the kids' tuition fees in school, and even save a little bit for the future. It was a sacred moment in my life when I told my brother that I no longer needed his support. I finally made it as a responsible adult in my own eyes and could not have been happier.

3—Improve Your Earning Potential, With Some Help, if Needed

When you start your journey as a first time breadwinner, it is very hard to believe you have what it takes. But remember every earning individual started somewhere and you are at that starting point. So do not look down upon yourself. Do not remonstrate yourself about your inadequacies and your earlier life decisions or circumstances that led to you being a stay-at-home mom. You have what it takes. The biggest block to our earning and finding a job is ourselves. The biggest block to our earning is our own view of our potential.

One way of approaching this is to take some time and sit and write a list of skills you have used and become good at as a mom. You are a good multi-tasker. You are a good listener. You are detail-oriented. You meet deadlines. These are just some of the skills I am sure you have as a homemaker. There are other person-specific strengths you may have or have developed. You may be a good event organizer as you organized events for your children's PTA. Or you may be a good fundraiser. When you create this list you will realize that you have so many skills that the workforce is looking for.

Even as you work on strengthening your inner beliefs around your earning power, spend time and energy building it. It can be in the form of workshops, courses, certifications, degrees, reading books—whatever is needed to help you move from just having a paying job to starting a career that will help you earn and build an identity in one line of work. It can help you find your vocation. This is important so that you can advance and increase your income and competitiveness in the job market. It is also a huge confidence-booster.

Before my marriage ended, I had just been introduced to the world of computers by chance and I found it a fascinating area of knowledge. It was the time when computers were beginning to be used in offices. There were institutions that offered different kinds of computer courses. I decided to get a certification in the basic computer usage for office administration. So I borrowed about $50 from one of my close friends and completed the course. I now felt more confident in my updated skills and thought that would help me find employment. While it was useful in finding my first job, it also enabled me to launch myself into an IT career a few years later.

My client Vidya went through a similar journey when she had to start out earning as a single parent. Taking the first job she managed to get with the help of friends, she enrolled herself into a part-time business administration course (MBA) on borrowed money. She worked hard for two years both at her job and her studies. Once she got her degree, she switched over to a better position in another job that paid well.

My client Jaya also did an advanced certification in Pharmacology to enhance her qualifications while she searched for a full-time position. Her parents helped her fund the course. Getting the certification gave her confidence and boosted her badly battered morale from her acrimonious divorce.

So while you start where you are, you should consider renewing and refreshing your knowledge and skills at a suitable point. I know that funding such a project would be difficult for a late-starter single mom. If you can't fund it yourself, find people who believe in you who can help. Allow them to help you. That help can take many forms from funding a course to baby-sitting your kids while you study or go for classes. Don't deprive yourself of opportunities in the long run by not accepting help and support from those who offer it. Building your earning potential helps make you more attractive for employment, and, more importantly, the fact that you re-educated yourself serves as an immense boost to your confidence level. Your children will also be very proud of you.

4—Figure Out How Much You Need

When you were a married family, you might have had more than a comfortable existence. You may have had a nice home (though there was a mortgage), you had a car or two, possible household help for the home chores, cable TV, gym membership, and so on. As a homemaker you did not have to contribute towards paying the bills; you just had to manage the money flow. But now you are the sole breadwinner and the circumstances have changed. How much do you need for your basic requirements and what can you really afford?

When I was a child, home cooked food was the rule of the day and we never lacked for it. My mother cooked simple yet delicious meals. New clothes were bought only for two events—one's birthday and

Diwali, the Festival of Lights. Schooling was not free and we were in good private schools. Movies were once in a while, eating out was maybe once a month; beyond that, life was not luxurious but I did not long for many other things because I had everything I needed. I knew that as I grew up, money was not plentiful to waste or splurge. This was the value that was inculcated in me and it was my baseline for my financial requirements.

In my single-mom life, the first requirement was a safe home: a home in a safe neighborhood, among people who you would feel comfortable with, for yourself and your children. Since I had two daughters, physical safety was of the highest priority. So housing cost me nearly 50% of whatever I earned. During the ten years when my daughters were growing up, we moved homes four times, all for the reason of safety. Not that the neighborhoods turned out to be unsafe, but at first the homes had to be close to the school. Then later, when my work took me traveling for a few days, I also moved a little closer to my cousin's home, so the children would have family nearer.

Education for my daughters was the next highest in my priority list and my daughters went to a good private school. At the point of my divorce, I was earning every month the amount the school charged per quarter for every child. We managed because my brother helped. The commute expenses were minimal. The children cycled or used the public transport to and from school. I too traveled by bus and later used the company transport.

We did not have to buy clothes for at least two years because whatever we had was enough. At school my daughters had to wear uniforms, so that would be an annual expense but beyond that, not much. We had home-cooked meals thrice a day and the children had packed lunches from home. We had a landline phone at home (cell phones had not yet made an appearance) but we did not subscribe to international dialing. I would talk to my family in the US via collect calls. There was a TV at home, but there was just national TV and not much choice in terms of channels and hence not very expensive. We lived a simple life and I remember feeling content once I reached the state of meeting all our needs by my own earning.

So for you, the new single mom, it is important to work out what your basic requirements are: Do you need to pay for day-care for your child? What utilities do you really need and how much do they cost? Do you need cable TV? Based on your priorities, and also on what you can afford, assess what you really need to spend on and how much. Figure out how you are going to pay for improving your earning potential. Remember the guardian-mom principles about doing your best and not feeling guilty about the rest. So don't feel bad about your current affordability. When things start looking up, as they will, you can pander to some of your wish-list items. But for now, enjoy your simple life and strive towards financial self-sufficiency.

5—Manage your Money

You, my single mom, will reach a point when you are self-sufficient. It is then that you have to decide how money should work for you. When you have enough to pay for your daily and monthly expenses, how should you create and use a surplus? What form of wealth will be useful to you? These are things that you will need to ponder over and make suitable choices, so that you can make good use of your money. Below I share with you some tips to manage your money.

Saving is Important

It may have been my middle class origins or my home science education, but saving a bit for a rainy day was ingrained into me as a compulsive habit. Even when I was just a part-time announcer on the radio with an insignificant remuneration, I put away that money in our savings account. When I moved to Bangalore with a not-so-bad salary, I lived frugally and saved 10% of my salary via an automated account. That savings habit continued for a long time through my single-mom life and finally got replaced by investments much later in life.

It took me five years to repay my friend's loan towards the computer course and the savings helped. It saw me through my jobless state for four or five months in between jobs three and four. It helped me retain my self-respect and once I was supporting my family completely on my own, it helped me never ask for a loan from anyone ever again.

Budget and Track Your Expenses

Thanks to the home economics lessons, I also had a simple budget for the year. I knew when the children's tuition fees were due, what bills I had to pay, etc. Normal monthly expenses could be paid with my salary. Any big-ticket expenses outside of the regular expenses would have to be paid with savings or money from other sources. For example, we could not afford to take a holiday for quite a few years. So I saved specifically for one and it became possible. My budgeting and accounting were on paper and later moved to a spreadsheet on the computer when I could afford to buy one. I still use the spreadsheet format and it gets enhanced every year to suit my needs.

Build Your Monetary Capacity

Just like you improve your earning potential, you can also increase your spending capacity by using money smartly. You can save and put away money; you can benefit from gifts and windfalls and keep them aside; you can invest when you can afford to.

My client Radha built her monetary capacity the unconventional way after we had a few coaching sessions. In the beginning of our coaching sessions we explored the unconscious but ingrained traditional values and expectations that she had internalized that still had her in their grip. And through coaching she realized she could reassess her priorities and the resources available to her. She could make monetary decisions that would be useful for her and her children in the long run.

Radha decided to sell her jewels that had been gifted to her for her wedding. Indians venerate gold and having and wearing jewelry was and probably still is a matter of pride and status. Radha felt that she did not need to wear jewels but would benefit from having some easily accessible capital for her family. So she sold the jewels and got about $750. She smartly invested a part of this amount (saving the rest for expenses related to her daughters) in shares. In a few years, the shares came in handy to pay the down payment for her first home. So her investment made very good returns and was useful later. If she had been the typical Indian woman, she would have clung to her jewelry, but she chose the type of wealth that would be more useful to her—a home.

The icing on the cake was that the money Radha had kept aside for her daughters was also extremely useful for extra courses they needed to take to prepare for their college education. This again was a good use of the money. So don't be afraid to build your monetary capacity in nontraditional ways.

Your Monetary Values

Living debt-free was a value for me. So once I reached the state of self-sufficiency and had repaid the loan I had taken from my friend, I did not want to borrow again. At that time my life in India as a struggling breadwinner was uncomplicated by having no credit cards; I could only spend the money that was on hand. I lived within my meager means out of habit and necessity. Later, I did have credit cards, and from the beginning, I paid off the complete monthly balance. Living in the US today, credit cards are a necessary evil in order to have credit history, so that borrowing such as mortgages is easier to obtain. I still pay off my debts as soon as possible and not just when they are due. Old habits die hard, I guess. I also believed in Shakespeare's words from Hamlet:

"Neither a borrower nor a lender be; for loan oft loses both itself and friend." I was not in a position to lend for many years. Later, when I had some surplus, the times I loaned money to a person in need, I did that only when I was sure that I would not miss it if the money were not returned to me.

So think about what your values are around money and live in alignment with them.

From Job for Money to Job as Career

When you start your life as a single mom, the priority is to just earn; then you aspire to earn adequately. You sharpen your skills if possible. As you develop expertise in your line of work, you start having a career. You belong to a specialized profession; you create an identity for yourself outside of the home. This is a nice place to reach, for your current life as well as for continuing on when your young ones leave home. At this point, my dear single mom, you have made yourself more than just a breadwinner!

When I started my life as a single mom, I was only looking for jobs so that I could earn and provide. I was blessed that I also made a career in IT over time. I even had my 15 minutes of fame as an expert in my area of specialization. I found that having a career helped me maintain my identity and self-worth as belonging to a specific profession and contributing to it and the people who were part of it. So do aspire to have that career once your basic need of having a job to provide for your family are met.

A Word of Caution

During the course of my career I did experience the normal human tendencies of comparing and despairing. Once I had attained the goal of meeting my financial needs, I felt that my life had been normalized. That brought with it the comparison of myself with my colleagues—

on roles, levels, and promotions. I lamented my late start, this time without blaming my parents. That was when I tried doing a business administration course via distance education. I believed this would get me a promotion. In fact, I tried it twice without success. I could not manage home, work, children, and studying for two years. Or maybe I just did not find the course interesting. But I felt frustrated that I could not add to my qualifications to a level where, in my imagination, I would be on par with my colleagues.

Over time, instead of focusing on my past and what I did not have, I focused on my future because it could be what I chose. I stopped comparing myself to others. I chose to consciously enjoy my work and the people I worked with. I made sure I used all opportunities to learn. Sometimes I was able to create opportunities for myself that were not there before. And such openings were beneficial to my colleagues as well as to the company.

The strange thing in my life regarding my job is that when I had a goal of reaching a certain position in my job by a specific year (when I fell prey to comparing and despairing), I failed miserably. When I had number-based monetary targets, I never reached them. But when I focused on learning at work, doing the best I could, and enjoying what I did, I was rewarded in every way, including monetarily. I learned that my self-esteem did not have to depend on gaining position and power at work. I evolved my personal philosophy: "At the end of it all, my vocation brings me my salary and money. If I am earning enough of that for my needs and my family's, given that I enjoy my work, why should I bother about (not) climbing the corporate ladder?"

Please note, my dear single mom, that I am *not* advocating selling yourself short because you started working late. What I am telling you is to think about what is important to you at work and go after it, not what is the norm in your working environment. You have had a unique life and that gives you the strength to make your choices based on what *you* want, not what others want for themselves or for you. So hold yourself above the corporate culture and use your distinctive perspective to get to where you really want to be, not where society and social norms tell you where you should be.

And this is the word of caution I have for you, when you make yourself a career woman. Do not fall into the trap of comparing yourself with others and feeling that life has done you an injustice; remember your beginnings, appreciate how far you have come, and live by your personal philosophy towards your career and money. Enjoy the Super Single Mom that you are and do not descend to become a rat in the rat race.

Chapter Conclusion

While it is normal to feel insecurity, inadequacy, and anxiety at your late start, you have a powerful motivation—that of providing for your children. So stir yourself into action and find yourself a way of earning. It may be a humble start but you can and will make it to financial self-sufficiency. You will be able to meet your basic needs and later afford even your wish-list items. Save, plan your expenses, and manage your money wisely and learn to enjoy it in ways that matter to you.

Summary

- Start where you are
- Sharpen the saw if you feel the need to, and qualify yourself for a brighter future
- Accept help if you must but strive toward a debt free and self-sufficient life
- It takes time to get to a state of self-sufficiency; keep going towards that goal and never give up till you get there
- Make saving a habit
- Budget for your outflow and make your money work for you

- Aspire for wealth; but in the meantime, live within your means
- Jobs and career are like bread and cake; bread satisfies the hunger and cake caters to your appetite
- Avoid the temptation of comparing; be grateful for your unique journey
- Starting late to earn does not stop you from making enough and more

Questions for You

- What is your action plan to attain financial self-sufficiency?
- How can you improve your knowledge/skills to improve your earning potential?
- How much can you save at this point?
- What career can you and do you aspire to?

Chapter 6

INGREDIENT 3–THE POWER OF CONVICTION

"It's the repetition of affirmations that leads to belief. And once that belief becomes a deep conviction, things begin to happen."
—Muhammad Ali

You have recently been through a divorce. It was not a pleasant process. You are an emotional wreck. Depending on your situation, you are angry, full of blame for your spouse, or feel guilty at your imagined inadequacy that made your husband leave you and the kids. You are filled with regret at having all your dreams broken. Underlying all the emotions there is also a question that keeps humming in your head, "Why?" Why did this happen to you? Why did the marriage fail? Why didn't you take up a job earlier when you were fresh out of college? Your parents shake their heads and say, "It's all fate, karma." You are not consoled. You need closure with the past, but the answers are not coming. You need to move on but the past keeps looming up in your mind and sucks your energy out.

You have led a sheltered existence until now. Suddenly you have to transform yourself into a confident woman of the world, venturing the job market, knowing how to handle interviews and impress employers. Where will the courage come from?

Your child is sick and you want someone to tell you that she/he will be all right. You just want reassurance from somebody, somewhere. Who will hold your hand?

Conviction and Its Many Names

Some of us believe in an entity that we call God. Each religion has its own version of God, with forms to depict God or without. For others, it is the universe, the laws of life. Some others are just positive-minded, without being affiliated to any form of God. For the purposes of this chapter, I will use the words faith, belief, and conviction synonymously, to mean positive-mindedness. And what exactly is this? I fully endorse Saint Augustine's words, "*Faith is to believe what you do not see; the reward of this faith is to see what you believe.*"

This faith opened up paths when I thought I was facing a wall, showed me ways to solve problems, held my hand and supported me when I needed solace, and gave me courage to forge ahead in impossible situations. I would like to share with you how I developed conviction and how it transformed my life and some of my clients' lives.

The Birth of Hope in My Life

I was born into a Hindu family. Hinduism has plenty of Gods, each with special characteristics and powers. There are scores of rich mythologies and epics and I grew up on all of them. But for some strange reason, as a young adult, I was an agnostic. My views on God were: "You may be there, but I am here and we both are happy where we are." I did not pray and was happy to peacefully co-exist with God.

Then I married and life did not turn out as I expected. I did not know how to handle situations and people and let stress envelop me. When my girls were about six and eight years old, we visited my grandmother in a small town in South India. My grandmother was an admirable woman; she had lost her husband very early in life and had four children to bring up. As a widow, she had inherited the family's agricultural lands. Contrary to an Indian widow of those times, she worked hard and long to tend to the land as well as her family. I still remember spending wonderful times at the farm among cows, scorpions, and cockroaches.

During my visit my grandmother watched me, all sad and downcast and commented acerbically, "You seem to be so gutless; this will not do. You have to face the world bravely. Say these prayers for Surya, the Sun God; you will get the strength you need." And she gave me a small prayer book with the verses.

I was desperate at that time and was grateful for any inputs, so I started reading the prayers every morning. I did not know what to expect, but in a few weeks, miraculously my thoughts became clearer and I started getting ideas on how my life should be, from where I was. Instead of avoiding disagreeable altercations, I could face conflicting situations with more courage. I made stronger and more assertive decisions regarding myself and my children in my daily life, when previously I would have been passive-aggressive and fumed in silence. As I became aware of the stirring resolve, my agnosticism dissolved and was replaced by faith in God or Universe, in a power that guides you from within. I started and ended each day with a prayer.

Of course, like most people, I too prayed for things I didn't have, for my wishes and desires to get fulfilled. I wanted a happy married life, a strife-free household. Not all my worldly wishes were granted. What I learned was that God makes the right things happen and that might not be everything that you think is right or things that you think are your right. Slowly I converted my prayer for God to guide me with the right thoughts, feelings, and actions into fulfilling his/her purpose in life.

I would like to share with you this poem by an anonymous author:

I asked for strength and God gave me difficulties to make me strong.
I asked for wisdom and God gave me problems to solve.
I asked for prosperity and God gave me brawn and brains to work.
I asked for courage and God gave me dangers to overcome.
I asked for patience and God placed me in situations where I was forced to wait.
I asked for love and God gave me troubled people to help.
I asked for favors and God gave me opportunities.
I asked for everything so I could enjoy life.
Instead, He gave me life so I could enjoy everything.
I received nothing I wanted, I received everything I needed.

This poem made me realize the answers to my own "Why?" questions.

Living with Faith

Saying my prayers and having them answered did not mean that life was hunky dory all the time but the prayers showed me the light at the end of the tunnel—hope in the face of dejection. Prayers for me (and I say this to my clients all the time) are not about miracles happening but about building your inner stamina, strength, and calmness to handle different situations. It is a way to share your load with this entity that makes the load seem lighter and the victory achievable. There were nights when I went to bed disturbed and troubled, pondering over some problem that seemed insurmountable. When I woke up the next day, my thoughts were clear and the solution possible.

The day I came upon the Reader's Digest quote that I talked about earlier, that day was a great blessing in my life in clarifying my commitment to my children. It guided me with the guardian-mom philosophy that I effectively used to raise my daughters. It reinforced in me the power of prayer.

Faith gave me the strength to pursue every opening that came my way. Between my third and fourth jobs when my life seemed the darkest, one day I felt I had exhausted all the leads for finding my next job. I was very dejected and had lost all hope. But I continued to say my prayers. And that was when I got a call from a friend who suggested applying to an IT services company because he had attended a meeting and heard one of the directors speak there. The next day I walked in and got a job—the job that led to a long career. You could call it fortuitous or you could say it was the work of God or my faith paid off.

Similarly, belief in God made my efforts of bringing up my daughters as a single mom lighter, as I left home first and returned last in the evening. It made me believe that they would be safe at home and at school. It made me share my responsibilities of caring for my children easier as I trusted God to partner with me to take care of his creations.

And so in time, functioning with hope, optimism, and conviction became a way of my life.

When I began coaching my client Vidya, she was angry with God. She felt that she had been done a great injustice by the universe. During the coaching period, she slowly started healing and slowly reconnected with her spirituality. When she reached out to me a few years later to help her figure out how to deal with her son's college selection as he was finishing school, she mentioned how she had found the coaching sessions valuable in reviving her faith in the universe; her positive beliefs had helped her sustain an optimistic outlook and the energy to withstand all the trials and tribulations of her single-mom life. With her convictions strengthening her resolve, she had completed her masters in business administration (MBA) and was able to secure a better role and job. Not only did she have enough money for her family and herself for now, but she had also started saving some money for her son's college and daughter's further studies. While it was not easy to accept the limitations around which tier college her son would get into, given the financial limitations, she was full of gratitude that her life was so blessed. She said her son and daughter were doing well in school and were happy. Gone was the Vidya who used to remonstrate herself with unanswered whys, to be replaced by this Vidya, calm and content, confident and courageous, optimistic and full of energy. I knew then she could now be a mentor herself. Vidya's story is again an example of how you can use your deep convictions to propel you to powerful results.

Partnering with Positivity

If you do not believe in a God, I offer positivity as an alternate term.

Positivity to me is seeing the good in everyone and everything. And built and derived from that foundation I offer my clients and you, my reader, the practices of positivity. They are as follows:

- Be grateful for everything in your life—acknowledge that you are better off than so many others and count your blessings rather than complaining about what you may lack
- Be content with everything you have—feel happy with your lot, appreciate that you have many things that others might not
- Find a silver lining to every cloud—find something good in your adversity, look for an opportunity in your troubles, learn from your failures
- Wish everybody well—whatever be your situation, feel happy for others' good fortune
- Find answers from within when you are faced with questions—use your gut or instincts to guide you, believe in yourself

- Forgive yourself and others for things that happened or did not happen—understand that everybody is limited by his/her own experiences, including yourself; don't hold others responsible for your situation; learn and move on without self-flagellation
- Focus on your efforts rather than outcomes—understand that the result is not completely in your hands, yet do your best
- Operate from a premise of conviction and not from doubt—don't think about what will go wrong; rather, work towards what can go right
- Eliminate anger and inertia—garner courage to take action in a calm state of mind

Practicing positivity also means that you put yourself within the perspective of the whole world or universe—that you are but a speck amongst the billions of other divine creations and that your rights and rewards are a blessing and not an entitlement.

Some of these above practices of positivity that I encourage are harder to follow than others. They require constant reinforcement. They require awareness, understanding, and naming the barriers that get in the way of practicing positivity. But the key is to try to practice it. And the reason this is important for you as a divorced or recently separated single mom is because the aftermath of your divorce and the enormous new load on you as the breadwinner and single parent can get you down into negativity and hold you captive there unless you break free of its shackles with intent. Negative energies are detrimental to the human being in many ways and, in the longer term, can lead to physical and mental illness. What you now really need is a sustaining and healing positive force in your life. So make that a conscious choice and seek it actively.

As I was converting myself from an agnostic to a theist, I came across and devoured several self-development books—*The Power of*

Positive Thinking by Norman Vincent Peale, *The Road Less Traveled* by M. Scott Peck, *Think and Grow Rich* by Napoleon Hill, etc. These books offer a lot of inspiration to change your thinking to a positive mode in order to get powerful results. I benefitted immensely from these books because they supplied the sustenance to my optimistic outlook.

My client Lakshmi had found a job and was recreating her life as a single mom. She made a few new friends at work with whom she could share some of her life story. They would remark again in a typical Indian way, "If a person as nice as you has had to go through so many trials in life, it must really be your karma." And "your karma" was usually (erroneously) interpreted that you were stuck with what happened to you and there was no way out of the situation. Constantly hearing such things from those she knew reinforced negativity, hopelessness, and lethargy in Lakshmi and slowed her efforts to improve her situation. Such statements made her believe that unhappiness and strife were all that God had planned for her and she had to accept her lot in life. She gave up on things ever improving.

Through our coaching sessions Lakshmi learned to practice positivity. Lakshmi told me that after those conversations she would return home and declare to herself as part of her prayers, "I will use all the opportunities that my present life offers to set right my circumstances and create the life based on my beliefs and values." These affirmations positively reinforced Lakshmi's goals and desires for herself and her family. She stopped feeling hopeless and started taking action to improve her circumstances. Lakshmi became a database analyst, earned very well, and her daughters are doing well too.

The Miracle of the Smile

Let me now share what happened to me as I was searching for my first job. I was in the depths of despair, frantically looking for any openings that would give me the required break into being employed. My daily habit was to take the bus and go for a walk along the beach shore. That was my centering time, when I would pray and also plan for the day. One day as I was on the bus returning from my walk, I looked around to see where I could sit, and a lady beckoned to me with a smile to the seat next to her that was empty. Just as a courtesy, I smiled back at her, thanked her, and seated myself. As grim as life was, I didn't realize how wonderful it was just to smile at a stranger, and how rarely I did smile those days. The smile relaxed my face, made my heart feel lighter and brighter. If we look at the relationship between thoughts, feelings, and actions, normally actions are a result of the former two. But that day I understood that if you act positively even when your thoughts and feelings are bleak, it helps improve them. It was almost like the action influencing the thought, and it was a remarkable phenomenon! From that moment, I made it a point to smile as often as I could, at whatever or whoever I could. During my coaching practice I have shared this miracle of the smile with many a client. I have heard back from them how smiling helped them lighten their day and once they made it a habit, their whole outlook changed for the better and life too started looking up.

The Law of Attraction

My spirituality strengthened by leaps and bounds when I came across the book *The Secret* by Rhonda Byrne. I was on an international flight and the seats did not have individual TV screens but a common one every few rows. I happened to look at the screen and they were showing a book review. The book was *The Secret.* I was quite drowsy but something made me watch the TV screen. I was curious to know what they were saying about the book. Then I plugged in my earphones and started listening. I came to know that the book was about attracting positivity into your life. My interest perked up and I listened to the complete session. When I landed, I bought the book at the airport bookstore and read it. It is about the Law of Attraction. It says that you can desire anything in your life; picture what you want clearly, then believe you already have it and express your gratitude; and you attain it.

The Secret was revealed to me at a really crucial point in my single-mom journey, when I had to travel internationally for work, leaving my daughters back in India. I did not want to decline such work opportunities—my daughters were older teenagers and could take care of themselves—but motherhood by habit, especially with nobody else at home, made me worry about their well-being from afar. The most powerful message I got from the book was attracting positive things in your life by thinking positively and being grateful for them. The book helped me drive away anxiety about anything. I moved from a state of worry that my children were alone and had to be safe, to a state of excitement and wonder that they were alone and were doing an amazing job of taking care of themselves while I was away. Before the book my prayers used to be, "God, keep my daughters safe from harm;" afterwards, it was, "God, thank you for keeping my family safe and for all the people who are helping us in our lives." Since then, in every prayer, I express my gratitude for everything I have and seek. It has made my life so joyous and light. *The Secret* liberates from worry and anxiety. I recommend the book and the philosophy to everybody I coach.

Chapter Conclusion

When you started this chapter, you had many anguished questions. I hope reading on has helped you let go of the pain, guilt, and anger and made you free to move on. I wish that you embrace faith and positivity and that they offer you a perennial supply of the mental, physical, and spiritual energy you need. I hope you view your journey with optimism and all your difficulties as opportunities.

I can say with conviction and confidence that my life changed for the better once I became a believer. Paths opened seemingly miraculously because I could now see them. The more positive energy I channeled on my problems, the easier they became to solve. The light of conviction eased my spirit and soul and drew away the darkness and negativity. Conviction eased my single-mom journey in unimaginable ways and I hope you too benefit from its benevolence.

Summary

- Faith and conviction pave the way
- Practice positivity
- Your smile can generate the positivity you seek
- Be grateful for everything you have and invoke the Power of Attraction

Questions for You

- How can you let go of the remnant negative emotions from your broken marriage?
- Where do you derive your spiritual strength?
- What are some of the things you are grateful for?
- How can you reword your worries to positive thoughts?

Chapter 7

INGREDIENT 4—INTENTIONAL LEARNING

"Learn as if you were to live forever."
—Mahatma Gandhi

I have always loved to learn. As a child and through most of my adulthood I have veered towards structured learning such as courses, certifications, and diplomas. I love acquiring knowledge and enjoy the "Aha" moments when you experience the light bulbs going off in your head about some concept or the other. This is an example of formal education that you go through when you have to acquire knowledge or skills of a specific kind. I spoke about this in Chapter 5 when I talked about earning and increasing your earning potential.

It is easy to be intentional in your learning when it is packaged in a formal way. You have to spend time learning and then formally demonstrate what you have learned in exams, tests, papers, and presentations. You usually have a start and an end date and you get some kind of tangible reward for your learning—be it a certificate, an award, a degree, a license—or some kind of credential that you can then use to have people in your life treat you in accordance with this knowledge you have gained.

But there are other kinds of learning, from life itself—adopting new attitudes, opening your mind to new possibilities, learning to forgive and forget, to be positive in the face of adversity, to function as a leader for your children—there are so many lessons that one gains as a single mom and I treasure those equally. Unlike formal learning, where you get a certificate for attending or get accredited in an area that you may or may not get to use at all, the life lessons are easy to practice in your everyday living. And the great thing about this learning is that there is no start or end date. You learn all your life. How wonderful is that! Jiddu Krishnamurti said, "*There is no end to education. It is not that you read a book, pass an examination, and finish with education. The whole of life, from the moment you are born to the moment you die, is a process of learning.*" So what is intentional learning in this context? Does it mean we go around looking for things to learn about? How can we do that amidst all the hundreds of things to be done in a day? In this chapter I want to share with you what being an intentional learner means, why it is important to be intentional as a learner when you are a single mom, and how to become such a learner.

What is Intentional Learning?

Learning is an essential and integral part of being a single mom. It happens consciously and unconsciously. The fact that you are even reading this book and trying to adopt and adapt these ingredients to improve your life tells me that you are a learner. And there is so much to learn, so much you are already learning about. Intentional learning happens when you look at everything—the good and the bad—as a learning opportunity. You have an intent to learn and so are able to ferret out the nuggets from your daily life experiences. For example, when you lose your way going to a new place, you learn the route better. At the end of the day when your child asks for something and you snap back, and the child's face falls, you learn not to let your tiredness get the better of you. As a new employee, when you get appreciated for a job well done, you reinforce the skills and habits that got you the accolade.

Each of the above scenarios brings out an important characteristic of intentional learning. *Intentional learning is always progressive*, because you are treating every single experience, irrespective of how it turns out, as an opportunity to learn. You have extracted the essence of it and it has become part of your mental repertoire. Isn't that amazing?

Intentional learning is also proactive. You are quick to make out what worked or didn't and put that to use the next time. Contrast this with complacence or absence of learning, where you keep making the same mistakes over and over again and still the learning does not stick with you.

So intentional learning is deliberate and purposeful and you consciously and continuously seek it in all aspects of your life.

The Importance of Being an Intentional-Learner Mom

Most people tend to fall under one of two categories with respect to learning from life:

The first extreme is you hold on to what you have learned and then never sway. There is no room for new information and new learning. You treat things as black and white and expect your children to follow your learned dictates. You apply your learned thoughts/habits/behaviors/rules independent of context and never change and grow with time. This is a problem. Examples of this are usually social customs and mores from your childhood that you want your children to observe or follow.

The other extreme is you tend to forget the hard parts of life, gloss over things, and then repeat the same mistakes and wonder why your outcomes are not changing. Here, learning does not happen due to people forgetting what they have learned because their circumstances are now different. This is bad because it makes you carry on with bad habits and behaviors based on old emotions, assumptions, and thoughts that then negatively affect your children and you. This type of learning is commonly seen in people with lifestyle-related health issues, where once you get over the worst with medication, you don't learn to eliminate the cause. Instead, you go back to your old ways that contribute to a recurrence of the problem.

As a single mom, you can't afford to be in either category. You have a deluge of change thrust on you and have to learn and adapt to your new life and all that it entails. In this situation it is better to be an intentional learner and not feel the lessons are forced on you. You have to choose to learn from your past and make sure not to be held back because of it. You need to learn what works and what doesn't. You have to make your learning stick for as long as it is applicable so that you and your children benefit from your knowledge/attitude/habits even as you are flexible enough to learn them anew.

Being an intentional-learner is important because you can't let opportunities for you or your children slip by while the past holds you in its grip or you still have not freed yourself from irrelevant mental habits. Intentional learning liberates you from self-judgment and short-selling yourself, to move forward with courage and confidence. Your life as a single mom, and as a late-starting breadwinner, needs to be forward-looking and progressive and intentional learning supports that.

Who is an Intentional-Learner Mom?

Because every single mom comes with her unique set of circumstances and challenges, each intentional-learner mom will learn in her own way and seek sources of learning based on her situation, needs, interests, and modalities of learning. Thus, I will not prescribe a definition for the single mom to qualify as an intentional learner. The key point is that *for intentional-learner moms, every life experience is and should be a learning experience.* The words I would use to describe the intentional-learner mom are: open-minded (as opposed to rigid), adaptive, curious, non-self righteous, having humility, compassionate, forgiving, and loving.

When I was employed at the IT services company, I used all the opportunities the company offered in employee development programs. There were time management courses, classes on decision-making, and personal leadership and collaborative working programs, which helped me manage my life (not just at work) in a more intelligent, informed, and confident way. I also read a lot of Peter Drucker books on corporate ethics (*The Effective Executive* and *Managing for Results*), others such as *How to Win Friends and Influence People* by Dale Carnegie, and *Emotional Intelligence* by Daniel Goleman, to name a few. Obviously, I absorbed inputs from all these sources, made connections of all this learning to my daily life at home and work, and felt empowerment seep into my life.

My client Lakshmi used to say that she always learned to be a better mom when her teenage daughters rebelled against her dictates and unilateral choices. She said she finally learned to accept that—other than immoral or illegal activities—other choices were good for discussion and decision-making in a collaborative manner.

My client Lata, with some coaching exercises I shared with her, intentionally learned forgiveness. After four years of acrimony, she was finally able to forgive her in-laws' role in her married life. She reconnected with them and established a cordial relationship with them. Her children could then connect with their father's family and enjoy their grand parents' affection.

My client Jaya realized that she had to keep her negative feelings about her ex-husband Ramesh at bay when she talked to her children about their father. She intentionally learned how to do this through coaching. When she mastered this skill, she was able to tell her children that they would get different things from each of their parents and they could enjoy both their father and mother by doing different activities with each of them. The children could now enjoy an undamaged and unbiased relationship with both parents and they were better able to accept their split parents' situation better.

As you can see from my clients' lives and mine, you can be an intentional learner in your own way and benefit from learning in every aspect of your single-mom life.

How to Be an Intentional-Learner Mom

Life offers you many opportunities and inputs to keep learning and become wiser. But in order to learn from them, as I have said before, you have to keep your mind and heart open and receptive and not let old mental habits get in the way. I can think of a few common pitfalls that block us from becoming intentional learners, so here are three important principles that you have to remember and follow when you want to be an intentional learner:

- Don't strive for perfection
- Accept that you will make mistakes
- Know that you will need to unlearn, learn, and relearn various things in your life

Let me expand on each of these now.

Don't Strive for Perfection

The state of perfection, to whatever and whomever it is applied, comes with an expiry time; the perfect state quickly becomes obsolete because you have already realized what further improvements need to be done or new goals have to be set. Thus perfection is a myth. In the learning context, when you think you are perfect, be it your whole self or parts of your personality, you are closing yourself to seeing alternate or better ways to adopt and adapt. What also happens when you think you are perfect or need to be perfect is that you might judge yourself and/or others as meeting or not meeting your standards of perfection. So you are focused on the end goal of perfection and not on the learning to get there. As a result, your mind is again closed to the numerous opportunities and possibilities for learning along the way. Therefore my first point about perfection is to drop any ambition of having it, being it, or wanting it. Being an intentional learner means that your state of being is one of noticing and smelling the beautiful roses (your opportunities for learning) on the path and not missing them in your hurry to get to a rose garden (your destination a.k.a. your perfection goal).

However, as you know, one often *wants* to be the perfect mom and breadwinner. You have set your standards about what that means and are striving towards it day and night. Your perceived failure in your marriage makes you want to compensate and be the best mother for your children. There's nothing wrong with wanting to be a great mother, but you don't have to be the perfect one or the best one, again simply because perfection is ephemeral.

You want to emulate your co-worker's description of her home's morning scene (by the way, that is a two-parent household) and want the same in your home. It plays out like this in your mind: your children got up without you having to wake them, they got ready without your help, the breakfast and packed lunch are ready for them, and they are off to school leaving you to go to work. Instead, what really happens is that you are yelling for them to get up, their school clothes have been forgotten in the washer, the toast is burnt and your child has left his/her lunch bag on the dining table. And how does all this relate to intentional learning? Well, the goal of this ideal morning scene in your mind creates stress when things don't happen your way. And stress comes in the way of learning. It impedes it and stifles it.

So the first principle is to leave perfection alone and work towards creating a loving and relaxed atmosphere for yourself and your children, an environment where all of you will share daily reports, ideas, whatever—a place where perfection is not revered but doing your best is. In the Indian home, getting high grades in school is the goal for the children, but many of my clients began practicing intentional learning and taught their children this too. And what happened? The single moms and children were now better able to enjoy their education and learning. The moms were able to balance their perfect grades expectation with the value of letting the children explore their interests and shine in what they enjoyed. The children began learning what they wanted to learn, and explored and developed interests and passions for fields of study that they then wanted to pursue as a career as opposed to learning for the sake of a grade.

Accept That You Will Make Mistakes

Thomas Szasz said, "*Every act of conscious learning requires the willingness to suffer an injury to one's self-esteem. That is why young children, before they are aware of their own self-importance, learn so easily.*" Children learn because they are not afraid of making mistakes and their mistakes do not impact their self-esteem. Whereas we, as adults, are conditioned to evaluate ourselves as lesser when we make mistakes.

As an intentional-learner mom, you can't fall into the trap of thinking that making mistakes is stupid, and therefore you can't let yourself make mistakes. While navigating through so many new territories, and having to do it alone, you *will* make many mistakes. Make sure you don't repeat your mistakes, but acknowledge them, learn from them, and keep going forward. This applies to all areas of your life as a single mom—managing your home, raising your children, and working.

Apologize for your mistakes when they impact others, even to your children. I have done this so many times—when I lost my temper with them because I was tired, when I hurt their feelings because of my style of communication, when I misinterpreted their motives, etc. (I learned to evolve into a better guardian-mom from such episodes.) And when you apologize to your children, they are so forgiving and much more understanding of your situation than you are of theirs. You also offer a fine example of yourself and instill in them the value of learning from mistakes and, equally important, forgiving.

In most companies, as a new employee, nobody expects you to not make mistakes. What they appreciate is your proactive learning, owning up when you make a mistake, and making sure you don't repeat it. So allow yourself to be human and don't be afraid of making mistakes, but do learn from them.

Unlearn, Learn, and Relearn When Required

Remember that each of us is a product of our own past experiences at any given point in time. We always carry baggage from our past that forms the foundation of our belief system. But as you come across new experiences, evaluate the old ones and, if they are obsolete, don't hesitate to *unlearn* or throw them away and make room for new learning. What worked for you as a married homemaker may not work for you as a single breadwinner mom. You may have to adopt new habits, life style choices, etc. and to do that you need to give up or throw away old ways of being. All of this requires unlearning. Then comes learning—something I have already discussed, so I will not dwell on it here again.

But sometimes you have to relearn habits and practices. You stopped using them when conditions changed and you either found them redundant or hard to practice. Now you have found another or a similar purpose for them and so have to embed them back into your life. Often it is also about just reorganizing things that you already know in your mind and reusing them in a different way that is relevant to your new situation.

During our initial coaching I had taught Lata how to use a simple accounting spreadsheet for her home expenses. When she started using it, her life was simple and she just spent what she had on hand; there were no credit cards. But after a few years, when credit cards became popular, she abandoned the habit of recording her daily expenses, since the credit card statements provided the records and monthly reports were available and it seemed like additional work to maintain a spreadsheet. She forgot why she had started using the spreadsheet and how it had helped her. Soon Lata found that she could not figure out if she was spending more than what she earned, because of the available credit from her credit cards. The monthly credit card statements did not help her ascertain that aspect of her finances. When she sought my assistance again as a coach a few years after that initial period of coaching, we discussed her current state of affairs and she realized that she had forgotten about the spreadsheet. So she went back to it, made sure she did not have a large debt, and was able to manage her finances better.

Chapter Conclusion

Your single-mom life offers a whole new set of opportunities for you to reset and recalibrate your life. In addition to formal education, you can keep learning from your daily life and make it intentional. Mistakes will be normal, common, and many, but that does not have to daunt you. Since you know you don't have to be perfect, you can look forward to your single-mom life as an endless, exciting learning journey.

So the key message for you is you can learn at any age and from anybody or anything. If you have to learn, unlearn, or relearn—be it knowledge, mental habits, attitudes, perspective—to create a brighter future for yourself and your family, be an intentional learner and don't let anything stop you, especially yourself!

Summary

- You learn from both formal education and from life
- Be an intentional learner and look for opportunities in every experience—good or bad
- Abandon ideas of perfection, embrace your mistakes, and learn in every possible way

Questions for You

- Think of an example of practicing intentional learning in ßyour life
- What do you need to unlearn or relearn?
- What are some things you have learned from your single-mom life so far that you can share with others?

INGREDIENT 5—PERSONAL CARE IS PARAMOUNT

"Nourishing yourself in a way that helps you blossom in the direction you want to go is attainable, and you are worth the effort."
—Deborah Day

I think, as single moms, we put off things or actions that we can label as self-care. Our thoughts are always centered around the children's welfare. Sacrifice is the norm, self-care an abnormal activity. How many times have you put off taking a nap in the afternoon or over a weekend, using the time instead to cook something special for your kids? How often do you tell yourself that you can't afford a mani-pedi because you can use the money to buy something for your children? Do you recall the times you went to bed late because you helped your children do their homework? Do you even know what activities give you pleasure anymore, because life is on such a tightly packed schedule?

This chapter is about caring for yourself as a single mom. Why is this important? There are two main reasons: One is that everybody needs time for themselves, even you, single mom, who is a dad, mom, nurse, etc.. to your family. The other reason is *especially* because you are a single mom and everything to your family, any downtime you have will greatly impact your family, much more than a little time you take for keeping yourself rested and relaxed. Previously, as a homemaker, you may or may not have had time to get some "me" time. Now it is imperative that you do because your responsibilities have doubled and the toll on you has quadrupled.

What Exactly Is Self-Care?

I'm sure there are tons of books on the subject of self-care. For the purposes of my book and based on my experiences, I will say that it is having personal time for:

- re-centering yourself
- some kind of exercise
- a little relaxation
- people to laugh with
- an outlet when you are feeling low

Let's dwell a little bit more on each of these.

Time for Re-Centering

When you are a single mom (and this may be applicable even for other moms), you probably have a day like this: Get up in the morning, have some coffee or tea, fix breakfast (if it's not a cold one) and then attend to the children as they have to be made ready for their day. Then get ready for your day at work. Though it sounds logical and straightforward in my statement in serial order, many times it is a total jumble of all these and some other tasks as well. It is probably the busiest time of the day and it can be very chaotic. You are worried about the sick child, one part of your brain is preoccupied with the meetings or deadlines at work, your body is on auto-pilot doing the various activities, so it seems like different parts of your body are multi-tasking to the utmost.

Given that my children were in double-digit ages, what worked for me was having a little time for myself every day when I said my prayers and mentally planned for my day at work and home. Then I would be ready to face the family and all the unplanned stuff that jumped into the day. And the way I found that time was with a 20-minute walk nearly every weekday morning in a nearby park. This was my me-time and I would not surrender it for anything except really bad weather. Considering that I had to leave for work at 6:30 am to catch the company bus and return at 6:30 pm, being the first one to leave home and last one to return, I got up at 4:30 am and my walk happened between 5:30 and 6 am. This was my small window of peace and quiet before everybody else jumped into my day. This helped me remain sane. It was my spiritual time and exercise time as well, so served many purposes, something I appreciated much as a single parent.

What helped this happen was some back end planning and organizing. Over the weekend, I would shop for groceries and lay out a menu for the entire work week. I was in India and we subscribed to the concept of hot or home-made for most meals. So the menu planning helped save time and unnecessary stress during the week and I didn't have to worry or wonder what the next day's meals were going to be. It is funny that I forgot about this menu planning activity that helped me a lot, but when my granddaughter started school a few years back, my daughter, who is a working mom, suddenly reminded me how I did my meal planning. That's when I remembered it again.

You can find your own slot among your daily routine for some similar centering exercise. My client Lakshmi did it on her way to work, in the company bus; her commute time was about 45 minutes one way.

So in the morning, she focused on mentally planning for her workday and also catching a few winks. In the evening, she thought about her routine back home and got ready to finish the day's chores at home. Having such a time helps you to gear up or unwind in your own time, when the kids are not jumping in every few minutes with their questions and demands.

Different people do this centering exercise at different times. Do what works for you but do it consciously, being aware that this is your time to re-center and recharge.

Exercise

When you think of exercise, you probably conjure up pictures of going to a gym, wearing special tight-fitting clothes, using specialized equipment, lifting heavy weights, twisting your body into pretzels. Well, I am not talking about all that. What I mean by exercise for you, single mom, is some form of physical activity, which is not just your daily chores. My take on exercise is simply this: You satisfy your palate and stomach with food, you quench your thirst with water or some other drink, you breathe air without knowing that you do, but when it comes to your body needing some refreshing action and movement, you don't even acknowledge it, let alone satisfy it. So I strongly advocate some such activity every single day to nurture your body. It is a stress-buster and just like the power of the smile we discussed in Chapter 6, it releases all the toxins from your mind and body and helps you relax. And why not, when you feed your stomach every four hours, drink whenever, and breathe many thousand times a day?

I know that you want to exercise every day, but can't afford a gym, don't have time for a workout, and have too many things to do in a day—so how do you manage it? And you also want to lose weight, get back into or stay in shape, and your doctor tells you how exercise would help you with many other health issues you may have.

Again, in this chapter, my intent is to make you aware that you can't be a healthy parent for your children if you ignore your own health and wellness and if you can't make a little time for yourself. And would you not like to be a good role model for your children to lead a healthy lifestyle? So some options you could explore are: you can go for a short walk during your lunch hour at work with a co-worker, you can do a few simple stretches every morning or evening, or just walk up and down the staircase a few times every evening. It is not my goal to make you run a marathon or win fitness events, etc.—though if you can do that, it is really great.

So what is the bare minimum? There are two ways to feel you are exercising enough to nourish your body. One, you exercise with the goal of exercising, for whatever time you can afford. Two, you combine it with other activities such as playing with your kids during weekends, walking to the grocery store, or taking a longer route from the transport drop point to your workplace. For me, the 20 minute walk everyday was prayer time, planning time, and exercise time all in one. If you are able to exercise by combining it with other activities (method two above) for about 20 minutes in a day, don't worry if you can't have a dedicated exercise session.

Over time, you will start understanding your body and knowing when you don't feel good. I call this being in alignment with your body. This helps you be proactive and attend to it earlier rather than wait till you fall sick. This is like taking an extra dose of vitamin C when you get the sniffles and a pill when you feel the beginnings of a headache. I have avoided downtime many times by just being alert to my body.

Relaxation or Non-Goal-Oriented Activities

At one point in my single parenthood, I even had "relaxation" in my list of things to do for the weekend out of necessity; life was so busy and structured. So for you, my dear single mom, I say that anything you do out of pleasure and not because it is a requirement can be a form of relaxation. Watching a movie on TV with the kids, just lazing around, getting a much needed mani-pedi with some friends, reading a book, taking a nap—anything you enjoy—can qualify as relaxation.

My client Vidya made a monthly ritual of watching a movie or eating out with her children. This served multiple purposes. It offered a little recreation time; it was a special occasion for the children. It also made the children see their mother both as a person who worked hard and yet had time for enjoyment. It gave opportunities for spontaneity and fun. Most important of all, it helped them bome closer, made their bond stronger, and gave them opportunities to laugh together. This shared laughter and the stories and memories they created in her children and her made a huge difference in keeping the family together.

I love sewing. This has been my hobby since childhood. There was and is always a sewing machine at home. In my days as a single mom, once my daughters grew up and outgrew wearing clothes that I had made, I used to make curtains, pillowcases, and other household linen. I could sew joyfully forgetting the time and place, and it wasn't a waste of time either. So if you have a hobby and can afford it, make time for it. It can be very satisfying to the soul and creativity is always uplifting.

I could not afford vacations for all of us until my daughters were adults. So I accumulated my holidays from the office to the extent I could, and this came in handy later when I could afford vacations. My daughters joined school and university youth programs that gave them the opportunity to travel to places in India and even abroad. I too travelled for work and could visit some sights in those cities. So we managed fine, even with all the constraints of money and time, by using getaways presented by other kinds of opportunities.

Amidst the busy life you lead, make time for just putting up your feet and doing nothing or for what you just love to do. Of course, if you can practice yoga or meditate, that would be a really good way of relaxing and rejuvenating. Dancing works too, karaoke in the shower, or even some gardening—whatever oils your wheel.

People to Laugh with and Shoulders to Cry On

I realized the need for having laughter in my adult life quite late. This is the reason I want to make sure I reiterate this to you, my dear single mom reader. You might have heard of laughter being the best medicine. There are several anecdotes as well as formal studies that have shown that laughter has health benefits. I remember coming across the Norman Cousins' article on "Anatomy of an Illness" where he explained that ten minutes of genuine belly laughter made him sleep without pain. In recent years, I have witnessed laughter yoga classes where elderly men and women laugh loudly and that made me smile and feel happy. When you laugh, your head and heart become light and you feel more relaxed. During and after a good round of laughter, you have forgotten all your woes, your brain seems to have done a reset, and you can resume your responsibilities feeling recharged. So find people to laugh with, read a joke book, or watch a funny movie with your kids. It feels wonderful.

For most of my life as a single parent, I was very intense and a type A personality. I always carried with me lists of things to be done. For many years, my family was just my daughters and I, after my parents moved to the United States to live with my brother. I did not have time to make new friends other than a few at work. The time for laughter and fun for us was with my cousin and her fiancé who we met over the weekends. But it felt really nice to let my hair down, relax, and just laugh about things at work, at home, and in the world. My daughters liked to see me laugh and told me so.

My client Vidya watched animated kids' movies with her children on their monthly fun time. She said that after laughing in the movie theater, returning home for the chores did not seem so bad. If you ask me how you can laugh when you have so many worries, well, let go of your worries for at least a short period and find an excuse to laugh; when you make this a habit, you will find that you have to search for reasons to worry, not for laughter.

You also need a couple of people to share your woes with or vent your vapors with. My suggestion is that you don't share your sad or angry tales with too many people because then it just fuels more negative energy in yourself. You start feeling self-righteous and full of importance. But having people to talk to when you are low, confused, or sad—the kind of people who will buck you up—is really good to get over such situations more quickly and easily than if you try to do it alone. Sometimes it does not have to be your family or friends who you share your woes with. It can be with a complete stranger or a professional.

My client Lakshmi had to seek external help when she went through a short bout of depression during her single-mom life. This was a couple of years after her divorce, when she was in a good job and life was over the initial slump. For two years she had been very brave, summoning all her courage in taking care of her life and her children and working diligently to stabilize their life. But one day at work, she made a mistake and—though it was not a major one and she could easily correct it—she felt close to a nervous breakdown. Not having anybody to share what she was going through, she reached out to me and I asked her to make an appointment with a psychologist.

She told me that all she did was talk to the psychologist about her married life and her divorce and cried quite a lot, which she hadn't done in a long time because she was just facing and tackling everything that life was throwing at her. She felt immensely better at the end of the session. She went for a second session feeling a lot more cheerful and upbeat. At the end of it, the psychologist said, "There. You just needed to get things off your chest. You are fine now and you don't need to see me anymore." Lakshmi said she had needed the release of just talking to somebody who was not judging her and felt fine after she had poured out everything from her head and heart.

Understand that you need at least a few people you can talk to and connect with when you are going through your single-mom life. They need to be people who will not pass judgment, who will not prescribe solutions, nor spread stories about you. You just need a sounding board, a shoulder to lean on, people who will make you see the positive side of things.

Finding the Motivation for Self-Care

While in my mid-twenties, I was diagnosed with a mildly herniated lumbar disc. It was a very painful experience and I was bed-ridden for a week, needing help from my parents for our meals and for taking care of my daughters. Afterwards, I was quite determined that I should never again be so incapacitated. I learned about how to keep my back healthy and put it into practice. I learned therapeutic yoga and made it a daily practice. This meant that I had to mend my erratically creative lifestyle, where I spent most of my free time during the day and well into the night sewing clothes for my children. Eating the right portions and keeping my body trim became a sustaining goal. I learned swimming because it is a good form of exercise for bad backs.

Later, as a single mom, I knew that there could be no down-time for me in the sense of falling sick, with two kids to take care of. And I would not forget the earlier bad back. So I made it a sustained practice to spend a little time on myself even with all the multifarious activities to be done every day.

My greatest motivation for self-care was not to let my back get me down again, which would then impact my ability to care for my daughters and throw the extra burden of my care on them. During my single-mom years, I don't ever remember falling sick beyond the occasional headaches and colds. I would like you to find *your* sustaining motivation to keep yourself healthy and to try some of the ways of self-care I have suggested. It is this motivation that helps you keep your personal care a priority and enables you to become the best guardian-mom you can be.

Chapter Conclusion

Your single-mom life is stressful—which is all the more reason that you must not forget your welfare. Don't overlook your needs for rest, recreation, and fun. A little time on yourself will go a long way in sustaining your energy for the long haul. It will help you be energetic and cheerful for your children. Where there is a will, there is a way, and you will be able to make the time and effort to do just a few simple things to make yourself feel nourished and treasured. You are definitely worth it!

Summary

- Self-care is very important for you as a single breadwinner mom
- Take and make time for re-centering and exercise
- Spend time on non-goal-oriented activities and relax
- Have people to laugh with and lean on when you need them
- Find your sustaining motivation for self-care

Questions for You

- How much time do you spend on just yourself in a week?
- What kind of activities do you do for rest and recreation?
- What are your hobbies?
- How do you unwind?
- When was the last time you had a hearty laugh?
- Who can you talk to when you feel the need to confide?
- How can you motivate yourself to make self-care a priority?

INGREDIENT 6—EMBRACE YOUR REALITY

"There are two primary choices in life: to accept conditions as they exist, or accept the responsibility for changing them."

—Denis Waitley

What is your reality? Your marriage is over. You had a partner with whom to care for your children; now you don't. You had been a homemaker until now and you have to start earning for yourself and to bring up your child/children. You came of age with an education and a set of skills that your parents or somebody paid for. You still have that. You have other skills as well that you probably don't recognize yourself. You are facing a whole lot of life changes all at once and you have to get used to them. These are just the facts around your new situation.

But what are your feelings about this changed set of circumstances? They are certainly not happy. In the past chapters we have seen in detail your possible reactions to everything that's happening in your life, so we won't go over them again. But those emotions are coloring your view of your world. When you wear the victim lens, you feel helpless and that slows down your efforts to rebuild your life and your children's. When you have your blame glasses on, you think everything around you is at fault and that makes you abdicate your responsibility for your life.

So what does embracing your reality mean? It means just this—taking responsibility for your thoughts, feelings, and actions and adapting to changing circumstances with a positive attitude. And why is it important? Why can't you go on living blaming others or feeling like a victim? It is important because the negative emotions you are going through will not help you start and sustain your journey as a single mom. They will not lead you and your family to a brighter future. On a day-to-day basis, they will drain your energy and leave you low in spirits. Embracing your reality, on the other hand, will empower you to face all the challenges, surmount all the obstacles, and reach your goals successfully.

How Do You Embrace Your Reality?

You can embrace your reality when you:

- stop feeling self-pity and blaming others for your life
- make a habit of looking at everything as an opportunity for you to become a better person
- understand that it all takes sustained effort
- realize that your choices need make sense only to you

For me, the joy of being in complete control of my life was so sweet that I would not have traded that for anything else. I was broke, being supported by my brother, helped by my parents, and the future was a question mark; but underpinning all that was a steely determination that I would, through faith, hard work, an alert mind, and the goodwill of others, turn around my children's lives. I would make it all work somehow, because there was no more dependency and expectations on somebody else to do that for me or even to share my load. I took on the job and was determined to see it through, as successfully as I could.

There were a few mental shifts that I needed to make during this journey as a single mom that helped me take total charge of my life. Let me talk about them now.

You Hold the Choice of Doing Something about Your Life

As a single mom, you are the leader. You hold your own destiny and can and should contribute to your children's. This is a great responsibility, and you have to equip yourself to take it on. Whether your single status happened by choice or not, you have your life in your hands. It is also an opportunity to create what you want out of it. You are no longer somebody's daughter, somebody's wife, but a person in your own right. Take it and shape your life and your family. In the past chapters you have learned how to be a guardian-mom, how to start earning, how convictions can create new avenues to prosperity and happiness, how life-long learning is possible and how it helps, and how important it is to take care of yourself; so use your knowledge, skills and new insights to good use. Envision your future, find your path, and go for it!

Shed Self-Pity

When I realized that my married life was not working as I had expected and hoped it would, I was in a state of self-pity and felt like a victim. Over almost half a decade I had mastered being the victim in my unhappy marriage. Though nobody except my immediate family knew about my unhappiness, I invited pity from others by getting recurring backaches.

It was then that one of my cousins—whom I had not seen for many years—visited and stayed with us for a few days. One night, as we were catching up on our lives, I lamented about my marriage and all the things wrong with it. He listened patiently and finally said, “Why are you so full of self-pity? You have an able body and a smart brain, so why don’t you get a job and do something about your life?” For me, those words were a rude shock! Me, full of self-pity? That couldn’t be true! Wasn’t I the sad heroine, who was dealing with so much, with nobody to rescue her? But those words jolted me and served as the turning point in my life. In a few days, I was filled with a grim resolve to find a job, start earning, and work towards having a self-sufficient family. I was done accepting the life of depending on others for our bread.

Eliminate Blame

Blame is the active version of shifting responsibility while self-pity is the passive version. In both, you avoid taking on responsibility. Feeling these emotions is normal, especially when you have been recently divorced and are struggling to make your living. Everything seems unfair and not right. Feeling angry, righteous, upset—all this gave a surge of energy to get some things done. But these feeling get in the way of taking charge of your life and are wasteful of your time and, more importantly, your energy. Instead, accept what is and take your life forward. You have the chance to live in the present and build your future. So let the baggage of the past go.

In my life, I kept blaming my parents for my lack of a career at the start of my life as a single mom. I spoke to them harshly about it while I was looking for jobs. It was much later, after my parents moved to the United States, that I learned to let go of blame and anger. What was instrumental in this was a three-day workshop that I attended via my company. The workshop dwelt on the spiritual side of life. In the first session, the trainer asked, “How many of you are angry with your parents?” Of course, my hand was raised, along with 90% of the attendees. The next question was, “How many of your parents are no more?" About 50% of the hands were still raised. Then the trainer said, "So most of us are angry with our parents and many of us, even after they are dead." That was appalling! The trainer continued, "Shall we start first with forgiveness—forgiving them for what they did or didn't do—and then ourselves for being angry with them? Let us replace the anger with resolve, that from this moment onward our life is our own." That was the turning point in my life, when it dawned on me that I now had my life in my hands but was still harboring anger towards my parents. I cried (as did most of us in the program), and felt the anger dissolve in my tears. After the program was over, I wrote a very long letter to my parents, apologizing for all my harsh words and requesting them to forgive me. That action cleared up the past for all of us and we were all happy to start afresh on a clean state. I found that it was so much nicer to love and be loved than to feel angry.

Change Yourself First

Reinhold Niebuhr wrote, "*God grant me the serenity to accept the things I cannot change, the courage to change the things I can, and the wisdom to know the difference*." You can apply these words to both situations and people. While you can't be responsible for what happens to you—the external forces—you can certainly control your responses to them and find opportunities to make use of those exact circumstances in your favor.

Niebuhr's words have helped me most in dealing with human beings. Many times, we try to change others because we think we are right and they are wrong. As a single parent, I found that my younger daughter felt let down by me several times. She thought that I loved her older sister more. No amount of explaining could change her opinion that I treated her differently and unfairly, until I used Niebuhr's principle. I had to accept that her feelings were real to her (and to me). All that I could do was to receive her communications calmly and continue to be the loving mom I claimed to be. I also learned to be open-minded to her ideas and actually found that her questioning of my decisions helped me become a better parent and person. Over time, the relationship improved. I could not change her to my thinking by arguing or explaining but when I made up my mind to be receptive to what she was saying, things became better.

Don't Assume Anything Will Be or Was Ever Supposed to Be Easy

For most of us, life is all about what we want. As a single mom, when you are starting your job, your career, it is like rock bottom and there is nowhere to go but up. But when things improve, your wants also increase. You begin to dislike it when things don't always go your way. The unspoken and unconscious expectation in humans (including me) is that everything should go the way you want it to. And you react adversely—mentally and physically—when it doesn't. It is in this state that you have to remember that nothing in this life is easy and that you have to keep putting in the efforts to achieve what you want, regardless of the outcome. And learn to enjoy the work you are putting in, which then lightens the load.

My client Preeti, during her first few coaching sessions, was full of complaints. She said her new job was so far away and the commute took so long; the day care that her son went to was not feeding him properly; she was too tired during the weekends so the house did not get cleaned, etc. I let her vent her frustrations a bit and then asked her "Why do we expect life to be easy and only comfortable? Who said it would be easy?" Preeti told me that as she heard the words she felt shocked. She had come to our session bemoaning her situation, her mind complaining about everything she had to do in a day. When she heard those words, they struck her powerfully, and she realized that she couldn't expect her life to be handed over on a platter, but that she had to put in her best efforts. Preeti said that it was a turning point in her new life; she lost her self-pity and was actually grateful for whatever she had and resolved that she would make her family's life better. She was able to open her mind to accept things as they came and keep her efforts going, without cringing, complaining, and being disappointed when what she wanted did not happen or happened later than she wanted.

Make Non-Traditional Decisions and Know That It's Okay

Taking full charge of your life also means that you sometimes have to make decisions that make sense to you (and sometimes to you alone). As a single mom, you have to make decisions on a daily basis regarding your home, children, and work. Base your choices on your realities and not on what others say or do. It can be very tempting to listen to your friend and try to ape her choices. But your reality is different and your set of circumstances is unique to you. So you can't take a leaf from somebody else's book and make it your own. Take inputs from others and make your decisions to suit your situation. Sometimes this can mean that you make choices that are off the beaten track. Even so, don't fret; you know what makes sense for you and your family. You don't have to seek validation from others who do not understand where you come from.

But how can you evaluate your choices for success? How do you know your decision will be a good one and turn out all right? What do you do when it doesn't work out? I had a very simple mental checklist to arrive at important decisions:

- What could be the best outcome of this option?
- What is the worst that could happen?
- Who are the ones impacted by it?
- What is your safety cushion if it does not work out?

Normally the outcome would be something in between the best and worst. If I could tolerate the worst possible outcome, I would choose the option. I would communicate and sometimes consult the people who would be impacted by it. It was a simple exercise.

You know that when I had started out as a single mom, I found a job in Bangalore paying me three times more than the one I had in my hometown, Chennai. So the toss up was between staying in the same place and having a slower start or jumping to a higher salary in a new place. Since Bangalore was not too far from Chennai, and considering that my priority was to earn to self-sufficiency, I chose to leave my daughters in my parents' care and work in Bangalore. My parents were not happy with my decision and urged me to rethink it. In my mind, it was very clear that this would be for an interim period till I could earn enough to have them with me. I would visit my daughters every other weekend and spend time with them. And if all this did not work out in three months, I would return home to Chennai. In this example, the best outcome would be that my Bangalore job turned out to be good and lucrative; the worst was that it wouldn't and then I would return home and had to hunt for another job. My children and parents were impacted by my decision, so I talked to my parents and explained the interim arrangement to my children. My children were comfortable living with my parents. I thought I could handle the possibility of returning to Chennai and look for another job or find another job in Bangalore, so went ahead with my decision to move. It made perfect sense to me.

Moving to a new place turned out to be a really good decision, in retrospect. It gave me distance, space, and time to recreate my life without the past creeping into my life in the form of well-meaning relatives, friends, and acquaintances.

Another example of a non-traditional decision is my client Lakshmi choosing to sell her wedding jewelry in order to have some easily accessible savings. You read about it in Chapter 4. Here I would just like to point out the way her thought process worked. At the point of starting her life as a single parent, Lakshmi thought that her jewels would serve no purpose as gold and precious stones, but as cash, could give her and her children more security. She thought if and when she needed jewelry later in her life, she could buy them then. Since the ornaments were hers, she did not need anybody's permission to sell them. She planned to invest the money she got by selling the jewelry in shares. The worst that could happen was that her investment would go bust. The people who would be adversely impacted were her children. So she decided to split the money from the sale in three equal parts—one for each daughter and one for herself. She invested hers and created deposits for theirs. This way, she de-risked losing the entire amount and safeguarded her daughters' interests. Her shares did well and her investment saw manifold returns.

I have successfully used this simple decision-making checklist every single time I have had to weigh the pros and cons of a particular decision in my life.

Chapter Conclusion

At the point of starting your single-mom life, life may look bleak. But instead of succumbing to despair, hopelessness, guilt, anger and the whole gamut of negative emotions, make a concerted effort to shed self-pity and blame. Take the opportunity to recreate your life as you desire; use your physical and mental resources to steer yourself and your family to the goals you have set. Knowing that it will take time and effort, by not being afraid of making decisions, and by accepting what you cannot change while opening yourself to changing, learning, and adapting, you can embrace and enhance your reality!

Summary

- You hold your life in your hands and it is your choice to make something out of it
- Get rid of self-pity and blame; they serve no purpose
- You have the ability to change yourself before you can influence others
- Life is not easy; keep going and do your best
- Don't be afraid to make decisions that make sense only to you; learn when they don't go well and move on

Questions for You

- How do you want to shape your life and your children's lives?
- What can you do to shed self-pity?
- Who do you blame for your life and how can you eliminate it?
- In which areas can you create changes in your life? What are some of them?
- What do you think is hard in your life and how can you reframe it?
- What is an example of a decision that might be off the beaten path, but makes sense to you?

MENTAL BLOCKS ARE THE ROAD BLOCKS

"I think we all have blocks between us and the best version of ourselves, whether it's shyness, insecurity, anxiety, whether it's a physical block; and the story of a person overcoming that block to their best self is truly inspiring because I think all of us are engaged in that every day."

—**Tom Hooper**

In the past chapters, you read about the six ingredients that make up the RECIPE to your success as a single mom. My RECIPE is meant to help you overcome the daily overt and obvious problems and issues you face as a new single parent. Each ingredient that I discussed is intended to help you overcome the challenges you commonly face emotionally and mentally.

This chapter is all about what can and will get in the way of embedding and practicing my RECIPE. Some of the impediments you face in your life are external circumstances—not being in the right place, the timing may not be right, not having the appropriate resources (like money) or there may be things beyond your influence that will constrain you. As an example, you might want to do a course that will augment your qualifications and help you earn more, but can't afford it at that time, so you might leave it for later or, if you think it is of importance right now, you might request a loan. Remember the quote: "*God grant me the serenity to accept the things I cannot change, the courage to change the things I can, and the wisdom to know the difference*"? The external constraints are what you have to accept; find a way around them, or change your external circumstances.

In this chapter I focus specifically on the subconscious and internal struggles you have to overcome. This is much more difficult than say, learning a new skill or planning for personal time, because they are deeply ingrained mental patterns. For example, you find it difficult to face interviews because something inside of you keeps telling you that you are not smart enough; or you remember the last interview you did badly and worry that you won't fare any better this time. To overcome such issues, it requires you to first become aware of the block, and then figure out how to get such mental chatter to go away.

Many times the internal blocks are not even apparent to you. Your conscious mind will find enough reasons and rationale to explain why you can't do something that you need to. As an example, you only know that you keep putting off updating your resume; you have the children to take care of, so many things to attend to in a day and you are so tired by evening; so how can you find the time? But the underlying truth is that you are paralyzed by your own perceived inadequacy in your qualifications and the fear of your potential employer not finding your resume attractive. Thus a part of you may tell you that updating your resume is important while another side of you finds excuses for not doing it. The result of this is a conflicted mind and, ultimately, stress.

So you can see why it is important to understand such internal blocks; it is only then that you can recognize them as such and seek ways to conquer them. Often these blocks can be overwhelming and you are unable to follow my RECIPE for success without external help. Because these issues are strong and powerful enough, if you feed them with your negative thoughts, feelings, and actions, they will only grow stronger and take you down the rabbit hole of unproductive and at times hazardous ways of thinking and being as a single mom. Though these blocks are mentioned in the earlier chapters, here I will talk about them explicitly, so you can spot them easily and then seek help or put in the effort to overcome them. It is totally up to you to overcome your inner blocks and they can be vanquished.

Here are some common inner blocks that get in the way of your progress. These could be:

- fear
- emotions like self-pity and anger
- gremlins that keep saying you are not good enough
- limiting beliefs about yourself or your situation
- negative interpretations and assumptions of events and actions

Fear

When you are a single-parent breadwinner, you have to encounter totally new situations and people. You have not been exposed to these and it is very normal to feel fearful. Fear is the reaction to unknown outcomes and most of the time you imagine a negative outcome in some way. So you don't really want to face it and it stops you from taking positive action. But you may not understand it as fear. You may either explain away your inaction to other valid reasons (as we saw above) or just wonder why you are unable to muster up the energy to take steps forward.

Fear's cousins are anxiety and worry. They also keep you stuck on negative outcomes. Courage, on the other hand, recognizes that you fear the possible negative outcome, but, by using compensating thoughts and acts, you can still try the unknown. Mark Twain said, "*Courage is resistance to fear, mastery of fear, not absence of fear.*"

My client Jaya and her husband Ramesh had moved from India to Dallas after their marriage. Though Jaya managed to get her driver's license in the US, she found driving on the freeway nerve-racking because she was not used to high speeds. She was afraid of missing the exits and being honked at by other drivers. When she was married, Ramesh did the highway driving while she limited her driving to the 10 mile radius that she could manage by driving on the city roads, stopping at all the lights. Now that she was divorced, Jaya knew she could not avoid freeway driving. But fear was still strong in her. After a few coaching sessions, she garnered the courage. She did a practice run with her friend the day before her test. On her solo drive, she chose the early Saturday morning hour, when there would be relatively less traffic. She had the GPS on in case she missed the exit and she knew she could drive further down and come back. Jaya made it safely to her test drive destination, which broke her fear of driving on freeways.

So fear is only the anxiety of the possibly bad outcome. Once you prove that it can be safely done, fear can be conquered. This is true for any situation.

As a single mom hunting for jobs, you may feel acute anxiety while preparing for your job interview. It is really important that you get the job, so you want to do well in the interview. (You are focused on the outcome.) Then you think of all the negative *what ifs*. What if the bus is late in taking you to the interview venue; what if you forget how you should talk about yourself; what if you don't get the job? (Thinking of possible negative outcomes.) What if you tell yourself, "I am prepared for the interview. I will do my best. If, for any reason, things don't go well and I don't get the job, I will learn and do the next one better. I will find that job which is just waiting for me." Here you are making positive affirmations and these are moving your thoughts away from negative outcomes. Your anxiety lessens because any outcome is going to be positive for you.

Self-Pity

Pity, whether it is for the self or for others, is not a constructive emotion. It is a state where you limit yourself from any countering of the situation to make it better and think that nothing can be done about it. When you feel pity for yourself, you are glorifying yourself for not doing anything. It is so easy to feel sorry for yourself, whine about your misfortunes, invite pity from others, and get some gratification from that. Being a victim is effortless and therefore easier than having to take some action. But this is not a healthy place for you to function in. You have undertaken the great responsibility of your children's lives and dwelling in self-pity is pointless and takes you away from your purpose. You are better off shedding it and focusing on everything you *can* do for and with your life. Again, it takes courage to become aware of your ineptitude and change the course of your life.

Anger and Blame

With anger and blame, your negative emotion is directed outward at other people and circumstances. You are right, they are wrong, and your action is aggression. Anger takes up a great deal of energy. It contributes to the build-up of loads of unnecessary baggage over time that can corrupt the mind and heart, killing joyful living in the process. I have spoken enough about my anger at my parents for deciding what I should study. It took a long time to let go of the blame, understand that their motives were based on what they thought was in my best interests, and to realize that, in any case, I was an adult and had charge of my own life and could stop feeling anger towards them.

Handling Negative Emotions

As a coach, I always advocate that one should not make decisions out of fear or anger. When you are going through either of these emotions, your judgment is not at its best. You are seeing the world with tinted glasses and the glasses' color influences the way you perceive the situation. What is required is to become aware of these emotions and shift your thinking to more positive levels—looking for opportunities instead of fearing the loss of the current comfort, taking responsibility for what is happening instead of blaming others—and then making your choices.

Gremlins

These are the inner voices that have embedded themselves in you over time. They curtail your progress by reminding you that you are not good at something, thereby stopping you from taking positive action. They try to keep you safe and small, which means as a new single mom, you try to remain within your comfort zone and avoid facing your reality with purpose and confidence. And that is not where you need to be. Do you hear your gremlin telling you that you were not good enough as a wife and so you can't be good at anything you do? Does it tell you that you are not smart enough? By paying heed to it, you are short-changing yourself in your efforts to become a good parent and, instead of forgiving yourself for your less-successful attempts, you succumb further to the voice, "See, I told you so. You are not smart; you are not good at anything."

This is what happened to me in the early years of my IT career. My gremlin made me think that I was not qualified enough for my IT job.

To counter that, I did many, many certifications and it took me some years to find my niche in IT service management and to finally feel I belonged there. In my case—though it did not stop me from progress—if I had recognized what it actually was and where it stemmed from, I could have approached my career in a more planned and thoughtful way, instead of trying to learn everything under the sun. I also would have avoided the wasteful expense of trying to do a distance-learning MBA program twice and not completing it either time. I certainly could have used the money in better ways than on an unsuccessful degree.

Limiting Beliefs

Limiting beliefs are things that you accept about yourself, your world, or your life. This acceptance makes you think you can't do something since it has not been done before. For example, a woman of my generation in India could say that she could not get divorced because it was not the done thing among the middle classes. So she would continue to suffer her unhappy marriage. You could think, "Everybody in my family was an employee. So I can't do anything on my own." My client Lata thought so and so started earning as an employee of a beauty parlor. In a few years, she had the resources to run her own business. But she was doubtful that she could do well as an entrepreneur. After a few coaching sessions, she decided to move forward on her own. She started her home-visit beauty business, which took off and let her earn much more, in addition to giving flexible working hours.

Limiting beliefs could also make you choose traditional paths for your children and curb their own interests. You might not want your son to study a course in catering because you think that cooking is a woman's job and nobody in your family circle has ever done that. So you keep pushing your son into becoming a doctor, when the child is really interested in managing a kitchen.

You have to learn where your thoughts, feelings, and decisions come from. You can then overcome them so that life for you and your children can progress.

Negative Interpretations and Assumptions

These are very common in daily life. At the end of the day, you are back at home and at dinner, you ask your daughter how her day at school went. She snaps back, "Why do you keep asking this every day? Everything's fine in school." You feel upset and think that she doesn't love you. Or you blame it on your daughter spending the weekend with her father. You go to bed feeling miserable. In reality, your daughter might just be feeling tired. All that you need to do is give her time and space to get over her bad mood. Instead, you jump to a negative conclusion about her, yourself, or your ex-husband, all unwarranted, and your energy level goes down. So negative interpretations deplete your mental energy and you don't really need that. Not when you are a single mom trying so hard to be good parent and provider.

You also assume negative outcomes when you encounter one a few times. So you give up trying and accept failure in yourself or in the situation. You become despondent. As an example, you may have attended several job interviews and haven't yet found a job. You assume that the next one will also be a failure. So you go with a negative frame of mind and don't appear to be on your best mettle. Instead, think of each previous interview as a learning experience and keep sharpening your act in the interviews. There is definitely a job out there for you and it is just a matter of time. So reframe your negative assumptions as learning opportunities and keep trying.

Chapter Conclusion

Beware of internal blocks that are stalling you or stopping you from making progress in your single-mom life. They are not easy to discern by your conscious mind and they mislead you with very logical reasons and excuses. So it is also very easy to hang on to them. They require a lot of deep digging, sincere soul-searching, and a conscious effort to be unmasked. They need courage and tremendous will power to be faced. Now that you are aware that they exist in the form of fear, emotions such as anger, self-pity, blame, gremlins, and limiting beliefs, commit to freeing yourself from their grip, with help if required. Don't let them get in the way of creating your recipe for success. Unmasking and exposing them is well worth the effort because, once visible, they can be pushed aside and then nothing can stop you from forging ahead.

Summary

- Internal blocks are difficult to recognize and overcome
- Be aware of inner blocks such as fear, self-pity, blame, gremlins, limiting beliefs, and negative interpretations and assumptions
- Ask for help if needed to free yourself from inner blocks

Questions for You

- What mental blocks can you recognize in yourself and how are they stopping you from progressing?
- Which are the ones you want to take affirmative action on?
- What situations cause you fear, anxiety, or worry and how can you reframe your thinking?
- What is your gremlin telling you?
- What limiting beliefs do you have?
- Think of examples where you have let your negative interpretations or assumptions get you down.

CONCLUSION

"Single moms: You are a doctor, a teacher, a nurse, a maid, a cook, a referee, a heroine, a provider, a defender, a protector, a true Superwoman. Wear your cape proudly."

—Mandy Hale

Dear reader, we are at the end of my book. I assume that you have taken the time to read the entire book because you are seeking answers to questions and concerns plaguing you in your life. I hope my book offered you some useful ways of thinking, some realistic expectations to recalibrate your life on, some best practices to adopt, and a few actionable items to review and follow. I hope my questions for you at the end of each chapter helped you reflect on your life and circumstances to understand your attitudes and behaviors that are assisting you or stopping you from being a strong, centered, happy single mom.

Each of our lives is different; your situations and your problems are unique to you. However, the best part is that you have your life in your hands. The futile dependency on another person is over. What you do for yourself and your kids is up to you alone. That freedom—the liberation from having to depend on another person—is euphoric. So with that freedom, throw in responsibility bolstered by earning, sprinkle some conviction, add a bit of learning into the mix, season with a pinch of self-care, stir in ownership of your life, filter the blocks away (with or without external help) and voila! That's you, the Super Single Mom!

For me, I needed to be in charge of my life so badly—the alternative had been so unsatisfactory and below expectations—that every trial I faced, every problem I had to surmount, was worth it. I was energized to make my life meaningful and worthwhile for my family and myself. And I had the fortune of being validated by my daughters that my decisions had been the best for them and me, so I feel grateful that the universe showed us the path and provided the support along the way.

I hope the RECIPE I shared with you resonated well with you. I wrote this book to equip you with the tools to handle whatever situation your life now throws at you as a single new breadwinner mom. Above anything else, this book is about letting you know that you are not alone in your journey and you can do it! And while this book was not about the practicalities of how to write a resume or apply for a job or earn the amount of money you need, I hope it makes you feel ready to shine bright and be a star in your own right—as a full time, first time single mom and breadwinner.

To summarize my RECIPE, the ingredients are as follows:

R—Responsibility to Your Children
E—Earning, Earning Potential, and Money Management
C—The Power of Conviction
I—Intentional Learning
P—Personal Care as Paramount
E—Embracing Your Reality

This RECIPE starts with your children being your primary responsibility, the fundamental reason for your status as a single mom.

They are your most important clients and you have to learn to now be their guardian-mom. Money is the most tangible resource and your efforts are directed at earning enough of it to make your and your children's lives comfortable. Money helps you serve your clients well. Faith, learning, self-care, and taking ownership of your life allow you to bring up your children and earn. They help you directly and indirectly to do a great job as a single mom.

Faith serves you as the foundation of your belief system that you can and will make it. It gives you the abundant positive energy that you can use for everything else in your life. By opening yourself to learning, you are empowering yourself with knowledge, skills, attitudes, and mental habits that strengthen all your efforts. By taking time to nurture yourself, you make sure your energy is sustained and perennial. By approaching your reality with ownership, adaptability, and relentless efforts, you are committing and creating the bright future of your dreams.

You are also now aware of the inner challenges such as fear, anger, self-pity, inner voices or gremlins, assumptions, and negative interpretations and how they can stop, slow down, or impede your progress in shaping your destiny and creating the life that you want for your family and yourself. You know that they are sometimes invisible to you and that you need to watch out for them and seek help, if needed, to surmount them.

This RECIPE of mine became apparent when I had to rethink my approach to my new life as a single mom. I realized they were essential and a powerful source of strength and direction. I arrived at these specific ingredients as I coached, mentored, and guided many newly single mothers or soon-to-be single moms who needed my help and support. They needed to know they were not alone in their journey, and that it does get better. And it *does*, my dear reader. So I hope you take my RECIPE and adapt it to make it your own. Use it to nourish your life in the best way possible because the time for celebration will be soon.

Every single one of my clients was able to use this RECIPE and it helped them think of new ways to rebuild their lives. They used it to create a vision for their lives, formulate action plans, and identify course corrections. Each of them has told me—and I have always felt it through my life story too—that when you see your children become independent adults embodying the values you raised them with, when you build that identity for yourself in your career, when you achieve monetary independence after having nothing of your own, you will know that everything you did and are doing is absolutely, undeniably, and unequivocally worth it! So, I wish you good luck in your journey and wish you a life full of happiness. May all your dreams come true!

FURTHER READING

These are the books I have referenced in my book. I hope you can enjoy them too.

- *The Power of Positive Thinking* by Norman Vincent Peale
- *Think and Grow Rich* by Napoleon Hill
- *The Secret* by Rhonda Byrne
- *The Road Less Traveled* by M. Scott Peck
- *Emotional Intelligence* by Daniel Goleman
- *How to Win Friends and Influence People* by Dale Carnegie
- *The Effective Executive* by Peter F. Drucker
- *Managing for Results* by Peter F. Drucker

Here are some other books that I have benefitted from but were not covered in the book:

- *The 7 Habits of Highly Effective People* by Stephen R. Covey
- *The 7 Habits of Highly Effective Families* by Stephen R. Covey
- *Nudge* by Richard H. Thaler
- *The Peter Principle* by Laurence Peter
- *Iacocca: An Autobiography* by Lee Iacocca and William Novak
- *The Automatic Millionaire* by David Bach
- *Start Late, Finish Rich* by David Bach

ACKNOWLEDGMENTS

Gale, you made my dream of writing a book become a thought and stirred me into action.

Divya, without your inputs and guidance this book would not have reached the shape it did. You and Bhuv were both captive idea generators!

Rasika, your editorial inputs really helped polish up the book.

Gowri, thank you for championing my writing skills and for being my informal editor ever since I wrote something.

Christina and Carole, thanks for being my sounding boards during our morning walks.

Shelley and Jenny, my life has been full of serendipitous events and you both contributed to those in bringing this book to life.

Gale, Gowri, and Jayanthi, thanks for being early readers and offering your suggestions.

Divya A, you are always around for solving my technical challenges. Thank you for your patience and willingness to help despite your very tight schedule.

Angela, needless to say, your coaching and guidance to this brand new author was of immense value.

Maggie, Cynthia, Mila and the editorial team, working with you all has been such a pleasure. Thank you for your support.

To the Morgan James Publishing team: Special thanks to David Hancock, CEO & Founder for believing in me and my message. To my Author Relations Manager, Margo Toulouse, thanks for making the process seamless and easy. Many more thanks to everyone else, but especially Jim Howard, Bethany Marshall, and Nickcole Watkins.

To my (global) launch team, for accepting to be part of it and wishing me well in this book-writing endeavor.

My clients, the Super Single Moms, thank you for trusting me to help you in your journeys.

Mani, you helped turn around my life at a critical time and here I am, hoping to be of inspiration to others through this book.

Shai, thank you for your confidence that I would make a great coach. It motivated me to start my second career.

My friends, the Houston gang, you all have been part of my life while I transitioned from my IT career to Life Coaching. Thank you for your friendship.

To Sukumar, Jayanthi and my parents, who helped my family so much during my single mom days and in whose love I bask always.

To Indu, Akshay, Carrie, and Rasika, I am blessed with having you all as family.

Trisha, Aquayus, and Irya, I hope you read this book by your grand mom, when you are older.

To Sashi and Eash, for your friendship through times thick and thin.

Vasant and Bhuv, thank you for awarding me the Super Single Mom title. That's rich, coming from the sons-in-law!

To my daughters Nina and Divya, who were the anchors in my single mom life and who are now my best friends. Thank you for encouraging me to write this book.

ABOUT THE AUTHOR

Janaki Chakravarthy is a certified Life Coach, an Energy Leadership Index Master Practitioner, and the Proprietor of Possibilities 'N' U LLC.

Janaki lived in India for the first 45 years of her life. From being a broke homemaker, she became the breadwinner after her divorce when she had to raise her two daughters alone. During the course of a long and fulfilling IT career, she moved to the United States permanently in 2007.

Passionate about helping other single mothers take charge of their lives, and having mentored and supported many such Indian moms to successfully make this journey on their own, Janaki became a Life Coach to do this work fulltime. She is drawn to this work because she believes that it is possible for single moms to grow in their own careers while simultaneously bringing up their children to be responsible adults. More importantly, she believes that this journey can be made in a healing and happy way for the moms.

'From Broke to Breadwinner' is Janaki's first book where she shares her RECIPE for success consisting of 6 ingredients that guide the single mom to be a successful breadwinner and more. She shares her wisdom drawn from her life experiences and those of her clients to help the single mom reader know that she is not alone in her struggles, has resources within her to get her through, and can successfully make it to the other side.

Janaki currently lives in southern California. In her spare time, she enjoys cooking, sewing, reading, and practicing yoga and meditation. Most of all, she loves spending time with her family and friends, and playing with her grandchildren.

Website: www.frombroketobreadwinnerbook.com

Email: Janaki@frombtobbook.com

THANK YOU

Hello Super Single Mom!

Thank you for reading my book. I hope it has helped you see that you *will* make it as the breadwinner and beyond. I know you will use my ingredients and create your own RECIPE for success!

If you have any questions or want to chat with me about your single mom experiences, I can always be reached through my website at frombroketobreadwinnerbook.com or by email to Janaki@frombtobbook.com.

You can also browse through the other resources available to you on my website frombroketobreadwinnerbook.com. So bookmark this site and come visit me there!

Wishing you the best in your single mom journey,

Janaki Chakravarthy

www.TheMorganJamesSpeakersGroup.com

We connect Morgan James published authors with live and online events and audiences who will benefit from their expertise.

FOR THE
DEVELOPING WORLD
LIBRARY
FOR ALL
DIGITAL LIBRARY

CPSIA information can be obtained
at www.ICGtesting.com
Printed in the USA
BVHW032349301118
534513BV00001B/7/P

9 781642 790221